Uncomfortable Labels

of related interest

He's Always Been My Son
A Mother's Story about Raising Her Transgender Son
Janna Barkin
ISBN 978 1 78592 747 8
eISBN 978 1 78450 525 7

Yes, You Are Trans Enough
My Transition from Self-Loathing to Self-Love
Mia Violet
ISBN 978 1 78592 315 9
eISBN 978 1 78450 628 5

Trans Voices
Becoming Who You Are
Declan Henry
Foreword by Professor Stephen Whittle, OBE
Afterword by Jane Fae
ISBN 978 1 78592 240 4
eISBN 978 1 78450 520 2

Queer Sex
A Trans and Non-Binary Guide to Intimacy, Pleasure and Relationships
Juno Roche
ISBN 978 1 78592 406 4
eISBN 978 1 78450 770 1

Sex, Sexuality and the Autism Spectrum
Wendy Lawson
ISBN 978 1 84985 631 7
eISBN 978 1 84642 112 9

Life Behind Glass
A Personal Account of Autism Spectrum Disorder
Wendy Lawson
ISBN 978 1 85302 911 0
eISBN 978 0 85700 371 3

Uncomfortable Labels

My Life as a Gay Autistic Trans Woman

Laura Kate Dale

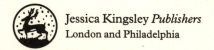

Jessica Kingsley *Publishers*
London and Philadelphia

First published in 2019
by Jessica Kingsley Publishers
73 Collier Street
London N1 9BE, UK
and
400 Market Street, Suite 400
Philadelphia, PA 19106, USA

www.jkp.com

Library of Congress Cataloging in Publication Data
A CIP catalog record for this book is available from the Library of Congress

British Library Cataloguing in Publication Data
A CIP catalogue record for this book is available from the British Library

ISBN 978 1 78592 587 0
eISBN 978 1 78592 588 7

Printed and bound in the United States

*Jenny and Ken Dale, thank you for supporting a child
who often didn't make life easy.*

*Becky and Makeda, thank you for being my Tres Horny Gals.
I couldn't ask for better gal pal nerds.*

*To everyone who has supported me, be it through friendship, engaging
with my work, creating fan art, supporting me financially or just
quietly reading and listening, thank you for letting me live the dream.*

Contents

————————

Part III Life Post-Transition and Diagnosis

Being LGBT and Having Autism Is Actually Pretty Common

When I was born in the autumn of 1991, doctors determined that I was born male. To be fair to the doctors, as well as my parents, it was a statistically sensible assumption to make. I was born with a penis, with no ambiguous secondary sex characteristics, and in the vast majority of cases that fact is directly correlated with someone being male. Most people born with a penis are assigned male at birth, live their whole lives comfortably identifying as men and think very little about their gender beyond the surface level. For most people, sex assigned at birth based on sexual characteristics and a person's innate gender are one and the same.

I was also assumed to be neurotypical, meaning that I was not identified as having any characteristics that would necessitate a diagnosis of a mental health condition or disability. Spoiler alert for the rest of this book: it turns out both those assumptions were completely wrong.

When I was just turning 18, I was diagnosed with Asperger syndrome, an autism spectrum condition now simply diagnosed under the umbrella term autism spectrum disorder. What that means for me personally is that I am at times under sensitive, and at times over sensitive, to sensory stimuli. When it comes to sounds, I struggle to filter out needless background noise from important primary noise, meaning in spaces with multiple noise sources I can feel like I'm being crushed under aggressive, invasive, distressing static that fills up my head. When it comes to nonverbal cues like subtext, facial expressions or body language, I'm under sensitive, and as a result, while I can with effort pick out those cues and understand their meaning, doing so requires immense amounts of focus, tiring me out quickly and leaving me exhausted.

In combination, these lead to me often being tired and overwhelmed by social situations. That doesn't mean I don't crave friendship, affection and human contact like my peers, but I have to engage with them in ways that accommodate my struggles. I can for the most part handle social situations, so long as I control the terms of the interaction and have reliable constants I can control as safety points; but sometimes it all becomes a little too much to handle, living in a head that's never quiet.

While there was no known diagnosed history of autism in my family prior to my birth, both of my younger half-brothers who grew up separately from me were also diagnosed with autism spectrum conditions, leading me to suspect the condition may run on my biological father's side of the family.

Also at age 18, I started to come out as a transgender woman to some close friends, meaning that while I was assigned male at birth, I felt there was a distressing disconnect between my physical body and the way I viewed myself on a core personal level. I felt uncomfortable about my body, I felt uncomfortable being referred to as male, and as soon as I switched to female presentation and pronouns and a new name, I felt inherently more at home with myself. In the years since I've sought medication, undertaken surgery and filed legal paperwork to change my gender on all UK documents. As a woman who is primarily attracted to other women, I tend to identify myself as a lesbian. Maybe I'm bi or pan – labels are complicated – but I sure as heck experience same-sex attractions.

So while the assumption when I was born was that I was or would grow up to be a neurotypical heterosexual boy, that whole idea didn't really pan out long term.

Maths time

I want to talk a little bit about statistics before we go any further. I know, maths is usually pretty boring, but I promise this little bit of maths is really important to what's ahead in the book. We're going to talk a little bit about how common being LGBT is, how common being on the autism spectrum is and how common the overlap of the two is.

In the UK, around 1 in 50 people are on Government records as identifying as gay, lesbian or bisexual in 2016,[1] and around 1 in 100 people in the UK are diagnosed with an

---

1   www.ons.gov.uk/peoplepopulationandcommunity/culturalidentity/
     sexuality/bulletins/sexualidentityuk/2016

autism spectrum condition.[2] Accurate statistics for how many transgender people exist in the UK vary depending on metrics used, with many transgender people not reporting their transgender status for fear of harassment or discrimination, but low end estimates are that around 1 in every 300 people in the UK is transgender.

The reason I bring up these facts is that while on paper those statistics would suggest being trans, having an autism diagnosis and being gay would be pretty statistically rare, there's actually a pretty high rate of overlap between the three. According to an international study by Dr Mark Stokes from La Trobe University in Melbourne, Australia,[3] a noticeably higher than average percentage of individuals on the autism spectrum identified as non-heterosexual, felt at odds with their assigned at birth sex, or suffered symptoms of dysphoria as a result of transgender status.

In an article in *Spectrum*, it was quoted that:

> Between 8 and 10 percent of children and adolescents seen at gender clinics around the world meet the diagnostic criteria for autism, according to studies carried out over the past five years, while roughly 20 percent have autism traits such as impaired social and communication skills or intense focus and attention to detail. Some seek treatment for their gender

---

2   www.autism.org.uk/about/what-is/myths-facts-stats.aspx

3   https://autismawarenesscentre.com/autism-transgender-gender-dysphoria

dysphoria already knowing or suspecting they have autism, but the majority of people in these studies had never sought nor received an autism diagnosis.[4]

The reason for this preamble is because I am a gay, trans woman with autism. In life, I'm often assumed to be a statistical outlier, a fringe case, and have to muddle together a bunch of disparate support structures to get by day to day. I attend autism support groups, I get help for my gender dysphoria, but never in my process of getting diagnosed with both conditions was the overlap addressed by the medical community. It was never pointed out to me that the two might share any links, that fixing one might help relieve symptoms of the other, and that I might benefit from understanding the areas where my struggles could overlap.

A statistically significant number of people, like me, are diagnosed with both autism and gender dysphoria, and there are a significant number of many and varied areas of life where the two intersect, clash, cause issues for each other and exacerbate each other. That's what pushed me to finally sit down and write a book.

I always thought I was alone. I never had anyone to tell me that my experiences made sense to them. I never had anyone else's experiences available as evidence that what I was experiencing was real. That's why I'm writing this book; it's the book I wish I'd been able to read when I was younger.

---

4   www.spectrumnews.org/features/deep-dive/living-between-genders

The book is structured like a memoir, following my personal life story from birth, up to today age 27, and using my own experiences as a launching point from which I can talk about the intersections between LGBT status and autism. The book is split into three sections: the first focused on my life prior to transition and diagnosis, the second focused on living through the turbulent self-discovery years, and the last more focused on life after things stabilised a little. That final section is a little less memoir and a little more personal essay, but it's still ultimately all about my experiences with autism and LGBT status, both the continued struggles I face and the joys I have found.

My hope is that by the time you're done reading, you'll have a better sense of how autism and LGBT status overlap, perhaps understand better why people in both camps might struggle to fulfil the stereotypes of how they are meant to act, and maybe know a bit more about how to support people like me who just want to get on with living our lives, even if we're a little out of step with those around us.

Trigger warning: this book mentions suicide
as well as drug/substance use.

I
_____

Life Pre-Transition and Diagnosis

CHAPTER 1

The Ignored Early Signs

While I wasn't diagnosed with Asperger's until the age of 18, and I didn't start to come out as transgender until later that same year, I struggled considerably with both autism spectrum symptoms, as well as feelings of distress and dysphoria surrounding my gender, from a fairly young age. As such, we're going to start my story right at the beginning, and talk about how I went so long with both my autism and LGBT statuses unnoticed by the world at large.

As a young baby, I simply did not sleep. Now, we're not talking the way all newborns don't really sleep; we're talking extreme-level sleep deprivation for my parents. While most babies will sleep for a couple of hours, wake for a feed and a change, rinse and repeat, I simply screamed and cried and refused to sleep. Ever. I slept through the night once aged eight months, then not again until I was well over three years old.

On a good night, my mother would be up around ten times in the night. On a bad night, perhaps double that, something that persisted for multiple years of my life. Initially my mother would get me to fall asleep by rhythmically squeezing my hand until I eventually dropped off. The problem was that once I fell asleep, so would Mum, who would then stop rhythmically squeezing, and I'd be right back to being awake and screaming. While it was not self-administered, this was the first recorded example I have of me being soothed by self-stimulatory behaviour, also known as stimming. The idea with stimming and autism is that, because individuals with autism like me are often overwhelmed by unpredictable sensory information, stimming is a way to introduce and focus on something that is predictable. In a loud room, I rub my hand or rock my head, and I know what sensory input to expect. I can focus on the known and the predictable, over the cluttered and unknown, and I find it easier to stay calm and relaxed. As a child, it's clear I already needed the comfort and security of predictable sensory information in order to feel safe and relaxed enough to sleep.

When it became apparent that the rhythmic hand squeezing wouldn't work, because I would wake as soon as the squeezing stopped, my parents would take it in turns to put me in the back of the car, strapped in a car seat, and drive around aimlessly, because seemingly being in the back of the car was one of the only things that would make me fall asleep for any notable amount of time. Looking back, I guess it was probably the gentle rumble that helped. Considering my later diagnosis on the spectrum, I'd guess that baby me was just a bit overwhelmed by all the varied sensory information that's present in a room that seems quiet for someone not on the spectrum. A predictable hum and rumble that drowned out other sensory information would eventually get me to drift off. Once I fell asleep, mum would leave me sleeping in the car seat for fear of waking me.

In a journal kept by my mother while I was growing up, she detailed one night where she attempted controlled crying as a way to get me to sleep. After two hours, she entered the room to find that yes, I had fallen asleep, but I'd also been crying so violently that I'd thrown up all over myself. Rather than clean me off, she just left me, for fear of waking me up. I don't blame her for that in the slightest; it sounds like she spent multiple years at the start of my life deeply sleep deprived, but that hopefully gives a sense of the fact that me not sleeping wasn't just some average baby waking up in the night stuff.

In hindsight, it's easy to look back at my extreme lack of sleeping in my early years as evidentiary of my being on the autism spectrum. It's an observed fact that people with autism often produce less melatonin than is normal, which when paired with sensory oversensitivity makes sleep difficult. The problem is, doctors and family members do not tend to take parental concerns of a non-sleeping baby seriously. Doctors often just suggest the same handful of baby sleep techniques over and over. Family members tend to dismiss the lack of sleep as a variation of normal. I'd argue that the fact I deprived my parents of sleep, to the extent that it was thrown around as an excuse in their divorce, suggests this was something abnormal enough it probably should have been picked up on. But it wasn't because first-time parents' concerns about their children are often dismissed as unnecessary concern. Indeed, my mum's concerns about my sleep were not taken seriously until she left me with her sister for a week. She warned her I did not sleep. Upon returning me to my mother, all my aunt had to say was 'I know you said they don't sleep, but I didn't realise you meant they DON'T SLEEP.'

This particular sleeping issue ended up lasting well into my adulthood, with me having to find ways to get around it over the years. Between the ages of 6 and 18 I would repeatedly listen to the same audiobook, *Harry Potter and the Chamber of Secrets*, on cassette on repeat. This not only helped to drown out the sensory information that was keeping me awake, and gave me something to do while waiting for sleep to come, but I ended up knowing the book well enough that I could predict what was going to happen well in advance, leading to it functioning well as a predictable sensory input. It was a sensory input that didn't end when I fell asleep, but would eventually stop itself when the tape reached its end. It ran just long enough for me: to fall, and stay, asleep.

As a toddler, one of the first issues I was able to verbalise was my distress at an inability to fix broken objects, an issue that has only worsened over time. As a very young child, if a balloon I had popped, I'd ask my mother to fix it for me, not to replace it with a new one, but to repair and fix the balloon. As an adult, I look back at those early experiences as a precursor to my issues trying to fix the unfixable as an adult. So, as an adult, here's how these incidents tend to play out. Earlier this week,

I broke a chain latch on my front door. I ran downstairs from my office to answer the door, forgot to unchain the door before swinging it open, and managed to snap part of the fastening, breaking the metal apart completely. When I break something, my brain creates an item, marked urgent, on a mental to do list. Fix that thing, you broke it, so now it's incorrect, and that's your fault and responsibility, so fix it right now. Sometimes, like the balloon or the door, it's not something I have the skills, tools or ability to fix. I had snapped a piece of metal, and I do not own welding equipment. Sometimes, fixing the item is just logically impossible. My brain really doesn't like that. I'll usually try to fix it anyway, repeatedly bashing my head against the problem until someone makes me feel abnormal for persisting, or until I spend so long on it that it interferes with the rest of my day.

This is where my brain starts to freak out. It's an urgent task, so I need to prioritise it, but it's impossible to actually complete. I know logically I should just replace the broken item, but replacing it isn't fixing it; it's still broken, and that's still my fault. Replacing it doesn't mean that it's ticked off as fixed in my head. At this point, the anxiety builds. My brain just starts getting louder and louder, more and more difficult to ignore. 'Fix it, fix it, it needs fixing, it's your fault, you did this, why isn't it fixed? You can't fix it? It's going to be broken forever because of you. That's your fault. Why would you do that? FIX IT.' My brain just shouts 'IT'S BROKEN THOUGH, SO FIX IT FIX IT FIX IT!!!!' over and over, until normally I end up having to hit at my head to dislodge the thought, as it just consumes me with anxiety and fear. I once experienced this because a loaf of bread, which can't have cost more than 75p, got squashed. It was in no way irreplaceable; my brain just couldn't get over the fact I let something break, and couldn't fix that situation.

Jumping to when I started school, when I was a little more able to communicate my needs, a lot of more obvious autism spectrum symptoms and diagnostic criteria began to surface, but ultimately went undiagnosed in spite of multiple in-school visits from the mental health service. Around age five, my mother recorded accounts in her journal of me developing a series of repetitive tics, which she could not seem to shift from my behaviour. I would tap my head as I walked, make beeping noises on a predictable basis, hop every third step, and every repetitive action she discouraged out of me was quickly replaced by another. They were always controlled, identical, repetitive actions, done consistently, and were more pronounced when I was tired or anxious. Again, looking back at my mother's early accounts, this phase of my life was me working out the self-stimulatory bit of self-stimulatory behaviour. This was me as a child realising that I could self-administer an equivalent to those rhythmic hand squeezes that had helped me sleep in my earliest days, at a time where I had to quickly learn to manage socially in order to cope with school. The head tapping was tactile stimming, the beeping was auditory stimming, the hops were action stimming; they were all serving a purpose, placating a need to know what was going to happen to my senses.

This was also the same sort of age my mother first started to notice and record accounts of me struggling with sensory information, even if her accounts didn't yet hone in on the fact that my distinct struggles were linked to each other. She made reference to me fidgeting with clothing, something I struggled to articulate was due to finding tags and certain fabric textures incredibly uncomfortable to wear. Tags tend to be made of a more rigid fabric than the rest of the clothing they're attached to, and stick out at a slight angle, causing them to be constantly pressed lightly into the skin. One of the reasons I specifically had fabric texture issues on clothing is due to the movement aspect of wearing clothes. If clothing is at all loose fitting, it tends to shift during movement, causing uneven textures to shift in unpredictable ways across the skin. As I grew up, I realised that clothing with fewer irregularities, as well as clothing that fitted tightly on problem areas of oversensitivity, helped a lot. Basically, avoid wool, and get sleeves and a neckline that sit well on the skin and don't feature tags. Don't wear anything with repeated numbers of seams, or anything that is made of multiple texture types.

From birth onwards I also really struggled with the sensory aspects of having my hair cut. I would scream blue murder, wriggling and writhing to escape the perceived torture being inflicted upon me. As an adult, I still tend to put off getting my hair cut, but I can at least now articulate why. One aspect is that my scalp is incredibly touch-sensitive, which is a pretty major barrier when haircuts necessitate someone touching your hair for extended periods of time. On top of that, as hair is cut, it tends to fall, leaving unconnected hair falling across skin, something which plays havoc with my oversensitivity. The light, ticklish sensation of hair falling, then lying on the body in an uncontrolled manner, is incredibly overwhelming for me. My brain tries to keep track of where it all is; I try brush it off, disengage from it, collect it together – do anything but leave it just lying randomly scattered across me. I can handle it now if I have to as an adult, but for many years it was a source of great mental distress, as my brain tried to keep track of far more at once than it was capable of.

Around this time my mother also noted that I had difficulty eating a relatively wide range of foods, for reasons I struggled to articulate well into adulthood. I know now looking back that the issue was that, due to texture oversensitivity, I really struggled to eat foods that featured more than one texture at a time. Picture pineapple for example. Initially it's a watery solid. Once you bite into it, it's suddenly a far smaller solid, and a huge amount more liquid appears. Then it's a gelatinous solid, containing chewy pulp in the centre. There are so many textures going on at once, it can quickly get overwhelming. At the time I failed to explain this properly to her, telling her I couldn't handle the texture of all fruit, to which she responded that all fruits had different textures. The issue is that while yes, fruit textures are all different, they all share in common the dual-textured nature that was causing me issues. It's also why I grew up eating my meals as separated sections, with one food eaten, then the next, then the next and no two foods sharing a mouthful. It all had to stay simple so I could process what was happening.

She also started to notice around this age that I struggled with undersensitivity when it came to temperature, wearing temperature-inappropriate clothing all year round. I would wear heavy jumpers in the height of summer, t-shirts in the dead of winter and many variations in between. I was ultimately unphased by changes in temperature due to undersensitivity, but highly bothered by clothing due to oversensitivity, and as a result wore clothes that worked that day for texture reasons, not for temperature appropriateness. To this day, I take baths far hotter than is recommended for the average person, because water of extreme heat helps me to feel the temperature in an enjoyable way that just doesn't happen with regular warm water.

I also struggled at this time with pressure undersensitivity, and found that the consistent pressure of water when swimming helped a great deal. I could also place my head under water, and quieten the world, which encouraged me to routinely swim long distances under the water.

Lastly, there's how my visual oversensitivity overlapped with my synesthesia, ending up in a story that took me nearly a decade to explain to my parents: the tale of Allergic Yellow. For those not in the know, synesthesia is a condition where some people's brains seem to get their wires a bit crossed when it comes to certain types of sensory information. For some it means sounds have flavours or numbers have temperatures; for me it manifests as colours having temperatures and tastes, which has been tricky for someone with sensory oversensitivity.

Picture the scene: I'm six years old, and our class is being taught about allergies. One of the kids in my class had a peanut allergy, and we are told that she needs to stay away from them because otherwise she'll feel very ill. It's at this point that 6-year-old me tells my teacher I am allergic to the colour yellow. At this moment my teacher panics, worrying I have an allergy the school has not been made aware of. My parents informed the teacher that, no, I was not allergic to yellow. Probably a decade or so later, I learned about the term synesthesia, and it all sort of clicked into place. When I see specific shades of yellow, my face gets incredibly hot, and I get this weird sour taste in my mouth that makes me feel ill and dizzy. I'm generally oversensitive to sour tastes as it is, and as a result the colour yellow used to trigger taste oversensitivity episodes in me. I get now what I meant, saying I was allergic to yellow, even if I lacked the vocabulary to explain it properly.

The thing is, none of these attributes were picked up, in spite of multiple visits from special needs assessors when I was first in school. I think a big part of this is ultimately tied into how both being on the autism spectrum, and being transgender, affected adult perception of my societal adaptation. You see, there are stereotypes about children assigned male at birth, and very few of them applied to me growing up. There's an expectation of brashness, over excitability, loudness and emotional closure, alongside a specific emotional range. These are obviously not absolutes, and many of these attributes may only exist because parents assume they're meant to exist and nurture those behaviours accordingly on some level. But the point is that I didn't line up with a lot of them. I was a quiet, shy, reserved child, who was sweet and did what they were told and was always in the right place, at the right time, doing what was expected.

Due in part to the prevalence of the 'extreme male brain' theory of autism spectrum conditions in the 90s, and the fact that clinicians had not yet shaken themselves free of the association between an autism diagnosis and perceived 'male' behaviour, my not fitting into traditionally masculine trait categories worked against me. Many of the more disruptive aspects of traditionally male stereotypes were in the 90s part and parcel of a clinician's willingness to diagnose autism, and because my autism presented in a way that was more in line with people assigned female at birth with the condition, I was just somewhat overlooked.

While there's not yet any firm list of differences between boys with autism and girls with autism, there are several observed differences in autism presentation that are now generally accepted as existing, and being overlooked by current diagnostic tool assumptions. These are not hard and fast rules, but some things that can make it troublesome for women to achieve a diagnosis. Girls with autism tend to have less trouble than their male peers socialising in their early years, but have a spike in difficulty entering their teen years. Girls with autism are more likely than boys to demonstrate a comorbidity with SSRI-treatable depression. Where boys with autism tend to be disruptive to gain access to physical items, girls with autism tend to be disruptive more often for human attention and contact. Girls with autism tend to be more passive, self-isolating and withdrawn, compared to boys with the condition who tend to be more outwardly aggressive. Girls with autism are also often more able than their male peers to follow pointing fingers and to gaze track.

While none of the above are absolutes, they are factors that are important, because they're all aspects of autism that applied to me growing up, in spite of my being designated male at birth. I was designated male, but was displaying more traditionally feminine expressions of autism. Pair that with the fact that twenty years ago these differences were overlooked by the male-focused diagnostic criteria of old, and you start to see how the diagnostic system overlooked me.

Thanks to the introduction of a predictable daily routine, something absent before starting school, I suddenly had a plan I could follow. There were places to be, things to do, and if I did the things I was expected to, not only could I predict what was to come, but I was also praised for doing so. I think that was kind of the problem. Because the introduction of routine and structure in the short term helped me to cope better with day-to-day basics, I was seen as functioning well. In some areas I was overly organised, almost to a fault, which when you're a young child is treated as a blessing in disguise. Looking back, the areas I was overly organised in were the ones built into my regular routine. If it was something that happened often, I overly planned for it to the point of distress if the plan was altered. In other areas I struggled to focus and keep my head on straight, but when you're a young child that's just brushed aside. There's nothing as a child that it's vital for you to do, so a bit of disorganised forgetfulness regarding one-off tasks that are not part of a scheduled routine isn't flagged as a problem. It was always unexpected one-off events I forgot to plan around or prepare for, because they were not a part of my day-to-day in the same way as the rest of my life. Nothing in those early years of school forced me to break from my routine too regularly, and as such I just got on with life.

I was able to fake social ability for the first few years of my school life, because lucky me, my obsessive area of interest and knowledge overlapped briefly with something that it was socially acceptable to be obsessed with. I became obsessed with the Pokémon series, the games, TV show and trading cards, just as it was becoming big in England. If I'd been obsessed with train pistons that might have flagged up as an obsessive interest, but because my obsessive knowledge-seeking centred on knowing the move learning levels, evolution levels and spawn rates of Pokémon during their explosion of popularity, I was briefly befriended at school by children who found my obsession beneficial. The problem there was that when their interest moved to a different topic, but mine remained on Pokémon, my social safety topic fell away and my social difficulties resurfaced as an issue. By the time I was struggling, the special educational needs officers had already visited, not offered a diagnosis, and set off into the wild again. I was seen as an exceptionally well-behaved child, because rules are structure and you don't go against structure, which was paired with me having a more stereotypically feminine emotional range and set of mental characteristics. I think the adults around me just kind of saw that as something not to mess with. I was a sweet, well-behaved child, so clearly nothing was wrong. My symptoms were merely odd, unusual quirks of a sweet, calm mind and a non-disruptive child, so there was no need to poke around and see if anything else was going on. Ultimately, the barrier to diagnosis here was that I wasn't disruptive enough to be seen as needing to change my behaviour, and was not put into situations that caused those kinds of symptoms I was experiencing to exacerbate to the point where they inconvenienced others. I wasn't stereotypically masculine enough to ring alarm bells to clinicians thinking about the extreme male brain theory, and I just slipped through the net. I clearly had the diagnostic criteria already, but they were not enough of a problem, in the correct ways, to be seen as needing help.

Transitioning to my relationship with gender

Switching tracks a little, let's talk about some of the early symptoms of gender dysphoria I presented, and the reason some of the early signs of my gender presentation were ultimately ignored.

I'll start off with how I personally know I am transgender, and what that meant for me as a child, versus as an adult. For most people, the physical sex we are assigned at birth based on a look at our genitals lines up with a few different aspects of how we interact with gender as a thing inside us that we feel and live with. Generally people are comfortable being referred to by the pronouns associated with their birth-assigned sex, they're comfortable with the majority of the social expectations and behaviours associated societally with their birth-assigned sex and they're comfortable with the physical body traits of their birth-assigned sex. So, for me to have been cisgender, a term here used to refer to someone comfortable with their sex assigned at birth, I would have had to be comfortable being referred to as he/him, be comfortable with the societal expectations that come along with the idea of masculinity and be okay with the body that being assigned male at birth left me with.

For me, that was not the case.

Growing up, I felt an intangible discomfort with being referred to as male, as a boy or being referenced with masculine pronouns. I couldn't explain why, but the terms just felt wrong, somewhat alien and disconnected from me. I also felt as if, in terms of societally expected norms, I fell more in line with how women in the world were treated, as opposed to men. While I initially didn't struggle with my male assigned at birth body, this changed considerably upon the onset of puberty for me.

While you can have people assigned male at birth who enjoy feminine-coded interests and that doesn't automatically make them transgender, for me it was the combination of discomfort with all three areas of my relationship to my birth-assigned sex that convinced me this was what was right for me. I was always uncomfortable being called a boy, I felt like I was more akin to the women in my life, and as secondary sex characteristics develop at puberty it became apparent that no aspects of living as male were working for me.

I knew from a very young age that I was uncomfortable

being referenced as male, and that I wanted to be treated like the women I saw in the world around me, but it wasn't until puberty that the pieces really fell into place.

My childhood struggles with gender

Looking back at my childhood, being a boy never quite felt right, in a way I struggled to really articulate until far later in my life. I was aware from the time I started school that something was different between myself and my male peers, but I was also aware that I didn't really fit in with any of my peers due to my sensory and social differences. I attributed much of my early gender-related discomfort to the same root cause as my struggles with social communication, struggles with sensations and struggles with conforming with my peers. I assumed I was just a little different, a little odd, and that if those sensory and social issues were not a big problem, that the rest of my issues must not be either.

I frequently found myself having the thought that I'd prefer to live life as a girl, without any quantifiable understanding of why. I wasn't yet struggling with my body; there was just some part of me that felt that was what was supposed to happen. I was aware I wasn't the same as the people around me, and I just assumed my discomfort with my own gender was the same as my struggles with autism, just me being a bit odd. With a lack of transgender representation in media, I had no examples of people like myself to look at, to help me put a name to the odd discomfort I suffered.

During primary school, a lot of the reason I didn't try to talk about my gender issues was a result of living with a younger sister, and watching the differences in the ways she was treated when compared to me growing up. My parents treated my sister pretty differently. She was given different social and emotional expectations, she was treated with a different level of attention and she was spoken to in a different tone to me, and all of those aspects of how she was treated felt more in line with how I felt I should have been treated. The support structures she was provided felt like the support structures I needed. The clothes she wore, the tone of voice used around her, the types of friendships she was offered and the ways she was addressed all felt more like what I was supposed to experience, and I knew the reason I was denied those supports was because of my gender. She had friends who got to laugh, share, hug and create. She had all of her creative ambitions nurtured and supported. She was given pocket money into her teens, where I had to get a job, because doing a paper round like me would put her at risk. The expectations on her were so different from the ones placed on me, and that only hammered home how different we were, and that I wasn't seen the same way she was. It hammered home that she was female and that I was not seen to be female.

I was a boy, and every part of my life was reinforcing that I was set to live a boy's life, and there was no fighting it. I didn't understand why I was being treated differently from a sibling I felt inherently similar to, in some intangible way. I tried at times growing up to break out of those gendered expectations, and make my parents see that I wanted to be like my sister, but ultimately there was a push back that reinforced that I wasn't allowed to escape the masculine mould, no matter how much I didn't feel like my male peers. I took up dancing several years after my sister, wanting to learn some of the grace and elegance that appeared to symbolise outward feminine expression, but I ultimately quit because my father insisted that if I didn't stop, I would be bullied by my male peers. When my parents made my sister a paper doll of a woman, with paper outfits which could be layered on top in order to play dress up, I asked for one too. After some discussion, my parents instead made me a Harry Potter doll, for fear I would be bullied and teased if I had a female doll to dress up. Both times, I didn't fight. I was already being bullied by other children for being different, and I didn't want to encourage that continuing or exacerbate it. I was different, and I knew that. All it took was a suggestion the bullying would get worse in response to me expressing femininity, and I quickly shoved that femininity as deep down as I could. Because I was already being bullied for my autism symptoms, the fear of being further bullied for expressing femininity, or rejecting masculinity, caused me to not tell people something felt inherently wrong to me about being male.

Once, when I was pretty young, a friend's little brother mistakenly added the letters 'any' to the end of my birth name, because that was how they thought names worked. They had a sister Bethany, Mummy, Daddy, and I just ended up with this 'any' sort of sound added to the end of my name. While it wasn't an explicitly gendered act, to me it made me feel like my name was being made more feminine, less male. I used that altered version as a nickname for probably a decade or so. I was just so enamoured with the idea of a feminine nickname that I had an excuse to start using.

On top of this, my biological father, who I did not live with, put a lot of pressure on me to fulfill the role of son if I wanted to achieve his love and support. He may not have meant to, but he did. At the age of six, for goodness knows what reason, my biological father, when driving me home to my mother and stepfather one day, told me that before I was born he had sex with a married woman behind her husband's back, she got pregnant, and that he believed that this woman's first-born son was biologically his child. Not only did he drop that bombshell but he informed me that my middle name was actually this child's forename. My father had literally named me after a potential older brother I might have somewhere in the world. As you can imagine, that was a *lot* for six–year-old me to take on board. My mother supported me a lot through that incident, and it ultimately instilled a strong moral compass point within me that ensured I would never cheat on any romantic partner in my life, but it did forever shape the way I saw my relationship with my biological father. I wasn't for certain his first-born child; I might be the second child, named after and living in the shadow of this older boy somewhere out in the world. My father was into football, sports, F1 racing and other traditionally male interests. If I wanted to live up to my namesake, I thought I had to be the son he had clearly wished he had raised. I thought I had to be male if I wanted his love.

Spoiler alert: unsupportive dads remain unsupportive dads, even if you try to fake an interest in all the things they like. He still didn't really seem to care for me, but I had to give it a shot.

When you combine both autism and dysphoria

Having autism, but being trans, medical staff looked past my autism symptoms because I didn't fit the extreme male brain mould of individuals with autism popularised in the early 1990s. By acting more in line with expectations of femininity, and more in line with female presentations of autism, there's a risk of falling under the radar as an odd but well-behaved child whose issues are not enough of a nuisance to those around them to be of concern. If you're trans but also live with autism, you're likely already a target of bullying, and parental/adult advice that rejecting gendered norms will result in increased harassment is taken very much to heart.

What you're left with is a child who knows they're unhappy with their gender, but afraid to say anything. A child who takes things incredibly personally and experiences the world at the extremes of highs and lows. There's a real clash, and for me, it was enough to dissuade transition and prevent diagnosis for well over a decade.

Theories that miss the mark

In recent years a few theories began to be floated around (often by those not on the autism spectrum) about why transgender status and autism diagnosis tend to be correlated with one another, and as someone who lives with autism, I'd like to take a little time to pick apart some of the ones I personally feel make the least practical sense.

One of the biggest theories posited over the past few years by non-trans medical professionals who do not live with autism has been the idea that people with autism are trans more often than the general population because people with autism often develop obsessive specialised fixations and interests, and that perhaps in some of us that area of specialist interest is gender, leading us to believe we are beyond the boundaries of gender itself or something to that effect.

Now look, I'm not going to try to deny that I sometimes have obsessive interests and that they can be a bit all consuming. Some of my first successful social experiences were a result of me having an encyclopedic knowledge of Pokémon, and I spent many years of my life dedicating my social life to organising and sorting trading card collections. But there's a big difference between how it feels to have an obsessive autism area of interest, and to be trans. When I obsessively fixate on a topic, I find myself dedicating my time to reading up every possible fact about it. Data, numbers, facts, solid unchanging information I can learn, and that won't change. I have a free moment and my mind will just shout a short four- or five-word sentence about that topic on loop, like 'exodia decks need card advantage and high turnover', obsessively thinking the same thought over and over and over and over to the point I'll make charts and write essays and re-read the same list of stats over and over.

I don't feel that way about my gender identity. It's not a

repeated, obsessive compulsion. It doesn't grab my head and shout, loud and frantic, repeating like a broken record, demanding to be fed, demanding to be allowed to show itself to the world. My gender identity is private and personal. It's calm, quiet and innate. It's a thing I know without research, and honestly a thing that in spite of its importance in my life has never demanded my obsessive looped fixation. I know I'm a woman, and day to day I don't think about that; I just know it. I've never read a book of stats about women, and I don't have any interest in knowing all the numerical data and points of information there are to know. It's just not the same as an obsessive area of interest. One of those is who I am. One is my brain looping and fixating and shouting until I'm full of static. Both are uncomfortable if ignored, but in such fundamentally different ways that the comparison only makes sense when made by someone looking at symptoms listed on paper.

There's also a theory that states that perhaps trans status isn't actually more common in individuals with autism than the general population, but only appears to be because autism causes people to lack awareness of social norms. The theory goes that, if lacking in social norm awareness, a person with autism who happens to be trans will have an easier time coming out, and that the rate of trans people in the autism community is actually more reflective of the general population percentage, if people were not afraid to come out.

As someone with autism who came out as trans, I'm personally not a fan of this theory, because it really downplays how tough coming out as trans when living with autism really is.

As an individual with autism, I faced decades of bullying and isolation as a result of the world being able to tell I was different, and I had seen the consequences of nonconformity first hand. The problem is that when you've already been harassed for not being normal, the idea of coming out as trans, another mark on you that will label you as abnormal, carries a terrifying weight: the fear that past harassment will occur again. I was brutally aware from media depictions how people react to gender nonconformity. I didn't want to repaint a target I had spent years trying to learn to hide. Coming out as trans wasn't any easier just because I was living with autism.

Let's also set something straight while we're here: I honestly can't work out how there are still people out there who believe in the extreme male brain theory of autism, in a world where so many trans women live with autism. How are there people who simultaneously think autism is real, and occurs in trans women, but occurs because those people assigned male at birth have brains that are too male? Are we so male we go all the way around to the other end of the gender spectrum? I don't think that's how any of this works. I do not believe I am so male that I feel female as a result.

Autism as a spider chart

One aspect of autism spectrum conditions that is often misunderstood is what it means for autism to be a spectrum condition. When many people picture the autism spectrum, they picture it as a straight line – from 'doesn't have any autism' to 'having all of the autism' – a strong to mild line that people fit on, and that binary line allows people to label the condition's severity neatly as 'severe' or 'mild'. When we talk about people with autism in terms of them being high functioning or low functioning, we run into a couple of issues. It overlooks the fact that there are people like me who might be able to function well in society for the most part, but some days I just have to curl up in a ball and rock and cry and I can't get anything done. I have high-functioning days and low-functioning days, and to distil my condition down to just one or the other side of that has its own issues. During the times I am read as high functioning, I am denied help and support for a lifelong condition I live with. When I am read as low functioning, I am denied agency over my life, and told I am not in a position to be trusted to make my own choices. Most notably, as will be discussed later in this book, gender transition healthcare specialists often attempt to limit access to transition-related treatments for patients known to be on the autism spectrum.

Autism's spectrum is far more like a spider chart, specifically the kind of spider charts you'll see if you google image search 'Persona 5 Stats Screen'. Don't worry if you don't know what it is, it's a video game; it's just the example I like to direct people to in order to visually illustrate my point. I'm on the autism spectrum, and when talking about my condition, you might explain it by way of a number of varying factors, each ranked one to five, mild to severe on that specific trait. I might be a four on audio processing difficulty, a one on speech difficulty and a five on difficulty eating multi-textured foods. Someone else might be a four on needing weighted blankets to sleep, a two on needing tags removed from clothing and a four on sleep issues. Rather than the severity of the condition being a single comparable number, it's a whole host of varied data points, which could be higher or lower from person to person. Sure, they might add up to a higher or lower number, but that fails to paint an accurate picture of the whole condition. Being nonverbal might weigh more highly than colour sensitivity in terms of hampering life, but that's not to say that a colour sensitivity wouldn't be terribly limiting to a person who loves artistic creation.

It's far too easy for people to visualise autism as a line from mild to severe, but it's ultimately a unique spider's web of difficulties and areas of ease which are hard to directly compare.

CHAPTER 2

Being the Weird Kid

From the ages of roughly 5 to 15, I was undeniably 'the weird kid' growing up. As mentioned previously, starting school, things were a little bit mixed for me. While getting a daily routine and structure to work within, and the consistency that was brought along with it, was initially helpful at getting on top of some of my autism-related struggles, that same environment required me to quickly adapt to a new level of social survival which I was certainly not prepared for.

So, let's start with the autism. It's no secret that children who grow up with autism spectrum conditions are often labelled by the adults around them as being 'a little different' or 'a bit odd'. Both of those phrases are couched in the politeness and softened edge of adulthood, trying to spin it as something not inherently bad. But, as a kid who grew up with those labels attached, I can assure you that other children are not nearly so nice, optimistic or forgiving in their outlook on the situation.

As I described in Chapter 1, there were a few years at the start of school where I managed to fit in okay, primarily thanks to an encyclopedic knowledge of Pokémon, which made me a valuable social commodity. The problem was that the fad level status of Pokémon only lasted a few years, and when it faded, my social status quickly faded with it and the other kids started to back away socially. At age nine, one of my teachers described me as 'being very aware of [their] limitations, including being forgetful, being distracted, difficulty with writing, and the many little habits [they] display'. That same year, I ate most of my lunches in the bathroom because I was afraid of being mocked by my peers. I was laughed out of friendship groups, and spent most of that year sitting alone by myself, watching other kids play, but not being invited to join.

The issue was that I didn't understand most of the nuances of social interaction beyond directly stated truth, with no hidden meaning behind it. I struggled to understand sarcasm or humour based on implied double meaning, causing me to take anything said to me very literally and at face value. I would routinely be bullied by kids who recognised this unquestioning nature and used it to their advantage. I remember being told by a fellow child that it was trade lunches day and I was supposed to give them the nice things from my lunch, and I did, because I didn't see why someone would make that up. There were kids who told me to eat dirt because that's how you got to join 'the cool group' and be friends with them, then laughed about it for weeks afterwards. I was coerced into doing things I did not want to do, because I felt cripplingly alone, and was too willing to believe what was told to me. The concept that I might be being deceived just didn't seem to occur to me.

On top of this, you have to consider that my disconnect with my gender impacted things too. When trying to socialise with girls, who I felt more socially connected with, I was largely shunned as a result of presenting at the time as male. Society builds up a set of gendered expectations around the way girls should treat boys as children, and those expectations prevented me ever being able to build those close female connections during childhood. These are all generalisations, but they're ones pushed by media, against children, that play a role in setting the barriers we place. Boys have cooties, boys are gross, boys are not to be trusted, boys are dangerous. Boys are not to be invited into the inner circle of a friendship, they're not to be invited for sleepovers, or sat with, or encouraged to think they belong. Any close relationship with a boy is romantic, and that'll be a point of ridicule, so don't get too close.

I really didn't fare any better when trying to socialise with the boys in primary school. Mostly, I was perceived as being too soft, bookish and overly emotional to fit in with what the guys around me were doing. I didn't have the right temperament, the right attitude or the right type of confidence. I didn't hold myself in the same way they did, and they could smell it a mile off. Over the years, there were boys who took advantage of this lack of confidence, assertiveness and support structures, most memorably when I was around ten years old a boy called Daniel. Daniel was the kind of boy who fulfilled a lot of the more traditional masculine stereotypes of what people imagine a young boy is meant to be. He was boisterous, energetic and knew how to work social situations to get what he wanted out of them. Daniel didn't live in the same town as me until moving there around age ten. Due to my clear struggles socialising, and my gentle welcoming nature, when this new kid transferred to our school the teacher assigned me as Daniel's first friend. I was told that he was going to be lonely, and I was mature enough to look after him, and that I had to make sure I made friends with him. Due to being on the autism spectrum, I took my teacher's command that I had to be his friend incredibly literally. I fully believed that, if I ever stopped being his friend, I would be breaking a school rule from a teacher. That's the groundwork for a lot of what came after.

Teachers and parents who talked about my friendship with Daniel often used the comparative phrase 'like chalk and cheese', a phrase meaning we were as different from each other as it was feasibly possible to be. We had nothing in common, and his energetic, rule-breaking attitude clashed deeply with my own personal values in a way that made me incredibly uncomfortable. In the early weeks, the only thing keeping me in the friendship was the insistence that I had to be his friend. Over time, the friendship shifted, into a form where Daniel took a far greater degree of control over my actions. The shift began a few weeks in, when Daniel began trying to test the boundaries and see what he could convince me to do on his behalf. He was the kind of kid who got into trouble on a regular basis, testing and breaking rules just to see where the boundaries lay, always to great discomfort on my part. That discomfort seemed to amuse Daniel. He enjoyed watching me fight to do what was correct and right. At first he was simply content to watch me squirm, refusing to break rules and getting uncomfortable. He would after a while lay off me, pat me on the back and insist it had been a joke, or some kind of test of friendship.

Over time, his approach began to shift. Daniel began to ask me to break school rules, and when I refused, to hold the threat of social isolation above me as a threat. I'd confided in him that I didn't have any other friends, a fact he manipulated over a period of around eighteen months. He would repeatedly state that he was my only real friend, and that if I didn't do as he said, I would be back to being alone. And the problem was, I was afraid of going back to being alone. He had given me a taste of social support. As tiring as Daniel was for me to spend time with, he was a person who told me that they liked my company. It was someone who made me feel like I was understood. Someone who made me feel wanted. That was hard to let go.

He took advantage of my fears of abandonment and isolation to strip me of my own name, referring to me only as 'stick'. He made me repeat a mantra, 'I'm as thin as a stick, so that's my name', over and over. I wasn't supposed to introduce myself by name to people if I was in his presence. He would demand I give him my possessions, and trade them for things he personally wanted. He would physically and verbally attack me, then afterwards tell me it was a joke, tell me that if I couldn't take a joke and told on him, I would be back to having no friends. Over a year and a half, he completely warped my view of social situations, by virtue of being the only person willing to offer me their social energy at school. He was the only person who made me feel reliably wanted.

He vanished one day out of nowhere. I heard his mother who he did not live with had taken him away in the dead of night. While I've reconnected with him as an adult, and he's apologised for the way he acted, his actions stuck with me for a very long time. I ended up using my relationship with Daniel as my model for healthy relationships for a while, and it kind of messed with me. Being socially isolated as a trans child with autism, it's incredibly tempting to take unhealthy sources of support, company and desire where you can find them. It's the reason I stayed friends with Daniel for years in spite of him beating and insulting me. It's the reason why I would often end up sitting across from my deputy headteacher, crying because I'd been bullied, and refusing to tell them who it was. I was afraid of being alone and unwanted. It's also the reason that, before I hit my teen years, I was on two separate occasions the victim of sexual assault from adults.

Without going into great detail about the specifics of either event, both were with older men who had reasons up front to spend time in my company, but manipulated my trust in them in order to do things that I look back on with horror. There was an adult who offered to learn to play the trading card game Yu-Gi-Oh, so that I would have someone to play with rather than playing imaginary games against myself. He later encouraged me to play 'strip Yu-Gi-Oh', which he very much led me to believe was a normal thing for a prepubescent child and someone above the age of sexual consent to do together.

He was eventually caught in possession of child pornography, something that took me a long time to process. My awareness of my own obliviousness took a long time to accept.

There was also a much older child on a trip away, one of the older kids who stayed with the group to help act as a responsible adult for group trips. He encouraged me to show him my genitals, in spite of the wide age gap before performing a sexual act which he insisted at the time was some sort of best friends bonding activity. He told me that, if he did it, then we would end up best friends forever. I'd never had a best friend. I felt deeply uncomfortable, but as he was the adult I was supposed to bring my worries and concerns to, I didn't know how to respond, and so I never told anyone. I just ignored him and hid from him as best I could the rest of the trip.

Both offered me companionship; they made me feel wanted, they threatened I would end up forever alone if I refused their desires and they made me feel like if I told anyone, I would lose them forever. I believed them, because as someone with autism I have always taken things very literally. Often, the idea someone might have lied to me doesn't even occur, and it's not until someone else points it out, or I get plenty of space and distance, that I can see I've been messed around with. When you're constantly alone, struggling to make friends but desperate not to be alone, you'll take any source of comfort that's offered, particularly those that manipulate you based on their knowledge of your isolation.

It took me a while, but I eventually found a support structure to replace those bad relationships in the form of my cats Ellie and Smudge. I've always liked cats; I feel like I have a lot in common with them. A gentle, feminine energy; a desire to initiate physical and social contact on their own terms; a comfort with being alone; but a need to have occasional social contact. Cats and I have a lot in common, and I've found them a pretty perfect level of social contact. Even today, my cat Smudge comes into my office in the morning, curls up on my lap and spends most of the day there. She provides warmth and pressure on my lap, which help keep me calm. She moves and interacts with me, offering a small living touch that just can't be replaced by non-living objects. She is okay with me taking time away without explanation, and she's there when I need to talk about the things I'm too scared to tell the world.

My first cat, Ellie, was the first living being I told out loud that I thought I might be trans. She was also the only one I wanted to spend time with in the immediate aftermath of getting my Asperger's diagnosis. She's a silent companion who doesn't make me feel odd, or weird, or abnormal. Ellie and Smudge offered me the comfort and support I needed to start growing away from some very unhealthy relationship patterns. It's thanks to Ellie and Smudge that I learned I could walk away from people who made me uncomfortable, or who hurt me, and I wouldn't be left alone and abandoned. I would always have my cats.

That sense of security is really important when growing up and later living at the intersection of two situations that often cause difficulty socialising and being accepted in social situations. They're a reliable constant, one that's not concerned with whether or not you're like the people around them. If you offer them love and support, they'll offer it in response. Sometimes, that's all a person needs.

Secondary school

These issues only got worse the longer I was in the education system growing up, as my sense of self-image became more solidified. I was a kid who was obsessed with specific niche topics that people didn't want to hear me obsessively waffle on about. I was a kid whose stimming actions to avoid becoming overwhelmed by sensory information started off as cute quirks, but over time became socially inappropriate coping mechanisms that were deemed optional voluntary actions that distracted other students. Sports were gender segregated, further solidifying the idea that I was not, nor was I welcome to be, with the people I felt more at home with. Bullies became more empowered and learned new methods to control and manipulate those they wanted to upset.

Bullies at the advent of secondary school started to target my coping mechanisms and take advantage of my obsessive nature. They would steal specific pens or items from me, and taunt me with the knowledge that they were mine but I could not get them back into my possession, and that they still existed but not in my company. They would steal or break stimming tools I had fashioned for myself, like a trio of magnets I would obsessively switch from a cluster to a line and back. They would tell me I was heading towards the wrong room or the wrong class, or that I was running late, in order to play with my obsessive anxieties. They would deliberately tighten my tie as I passed, making it incredibly distressing in its tightness, but simultaneously incredibly difficult to remove. They would spray water at my crotch alleging that I had wet myself, not to embarrass me, but because they knew creating a lie about me, and refusing to acknowledge the truth we both knew, was more distressing than anything else they could do. They mocked that I was too manly to be a girl, but too girly to be a boy, and that as a result I was never going to fit in anywhere. That one particularly stung.

One of the most annoying yet amusing things about thinking back on my childhood, as an adult who is now comfortably out as transgender, is the stark contrast between how I was viewed before and after transition, in terms of being perceived masculine or feminine. Put simply, every way I've ever presented my gender, the world has tried to tell me was wrong. The whole time I was in the education system, I was yet to come out as transgender, meaning in my school years I presented as male. Routinely, I would be told by adults and my peers alike that I was too feminine to be male. I cried too easily, I was too gentle and soft, I was into the wrong things, I spoke the wrong way, I held my body the wrong way or I socialised with the wrong people. It was a big part of the mentality used to bully me: I was too feminine, and that was a problem. I had to uncomfortably sit in gendered spaces like the sports changing rooms, afraid of my body being seen, and uncomfortably surrounded by the kinds of gross 'locker room' talk about women that you'll only experience when men think you're 'one of them'. I had to listen, and not be obviously silent, while also not agreeing with them, whenever they spouted gross sexist rhetoric about women. It was a hideous environment, where I felt I was being attacked without them even knowing they were attacking me. It wasn't a malicious attack, it was just what they happened to believe.

When I would come home crying after being bullied, my step-dad would tell me that I needed to man up.

Adults would look at my eyes, deep blue with what I'm told are exceptionally long eyelashes, and tell me my eyelashes were wasted on a boy. They were too gorgeous. Any woman would kill for natural lashes like mine. In adulthood, I've had makeup artists shocked by those lashes. In childhood, I was told they were lashes only a woman deserved, and that I didn't deserve them, as I was not a woman. I loved my eyelashes. I hated that I'd stolen them, forever to waste them on an undeserving male face.

Now, if you grow up being told you're not masculine enough to be male, you'll probably end up like me, assuming that if you transition, that clearly inherent femininity will shine through. Growing up, everyone could clearly see the woman underneath my male label, and as such surely if I try to present as female, that'll just be leaning into that, right? Unfortunately, it's not quite that simple.

As an out trans adult, I'm now told I'm too masculine to be female, which feels like the world playing a cruel joke.

Not transitioning until after I'd gone through a testosterone puberty certainly didn't help with that, as it's pretty hard to fight some of those changes once they've happened.

Still, nobody tells me anymore that my eyelashes should belong to somebody else. I like that I'm now allowed to enjoy my eyelashes.

CHAPTER 3

The Teen Tipping Point

Growing up, feelings of being uncomfortable with my assigned at birth gender, as well as struggles with the symptoms of autism, were both real and present parts of my life. I lived quietly harbouring an awareness that I didn't see the world the same as others, or feel at ease with who the world thought I was. The symptoms were visible, but I had them sufficiently under control so that they didn't cause problems for the people around me. My struggles were my own, and they were able to be kept isolated in my own little bubble, and so they were ignored by both me and the world around me.

That all changed when I was around 15 years old, when a series of life changes made both my autism and my trans status bubble to the surface, in forms that I and those around me found harder to deny were problems. Let's start with the first big change in my teenage years that acted as a catalyst for change: undergoing testosterone-based puberty.

When at around 15 I started to undergo masculine, test-osterone-based puberty it was noticeably later than most of my peers. It all began with my Adam's apple, which ballooned in size seemingly overnight. Due to my very wiry frame, my pointy Adam's apple was more prominent than was common, a fact which often drew comments. I vividly remember a dinner at a restaurant where my younger sister kept moving her hand up and down in time with my Adam's apple every time I swallowed, commenting on how weird and pointy and visible it was to the world. I ended up going and crying in the bathroom, pushing my throat, trying to flatten it. Then came the voice changes. My voice dipped fairly noticeably, and I instantly hated it. It felt heavy, weighed down and alien. It never felt like it fitted in my mouth. It was another person's voice replacing my own. However, my relationship with my voice wasn't terribly simple, because the voice drop coincided with a momentary drop in bullying.

A lot of the bullying I received in the early years of secondary school education centred around my gendered presentation, my not being masculine enough to be considered male. This being the mid-2000s, calling someone at school gay was still a pretty common insult topic. I got deeply frustrated by the suggestion, but not because I thought there was anything wrong with two people of the same gender being attracted to each other. What I struggled to verbalise at the time was a deep confusion around how the term gay applied to me. I knew I wasn't attracted to men, which was the root of their allegations, but I also knew that I didn't feel like heterosexuality fitted me either. Years later I would put two and two together that I was gay and attracted to women, and that was why the label of gay being used to pair me with men hurt. I wanted that term to pair me with women. I dearly wanted the bullies to stop positioning me as a gay man, because every time they did it forced me to ask myself uncomfortable questions about myself that I wasn't yet ready to find the answers to.

Returning to my voice changes, this was where that double-edged sword came into play. While I hated my new deeper voice, it seemed to very quickly prevent bullies from calling me a gay man as an insult. Sure they still bullied me, but it was no longer on a topic that forced me to confront very scary questions about identity, so I considered it a step up. This played in to how I ended up feeling about facial hair as it began to grow. I deeply disliked its presence, but it stopped people from questioning my gender in ways I was not ready to address. I worked out that I could grow my hair out long, but as long as I kept facial hair, nobody would suspect anything about my feelings regarding gender. My facial hair was a smoke screen, used to grow my hair out to a length I felt more comfortable with, while avoiding any tough questions.

Having lived through the 90s and early 2000s, I was well aware that trans people were the punchlines to jokes, not people to be taken seriously. *Ace Ventura: Pet Detective* featured a trans woman character, who the protagonist finds attractive, until learning of her trans status. He proceeds to vomit repeatedly and scrub himself, while crying. This is all played off as a gag. He then strips off all her clothes in front of an audience, much to her dismay, exposing her penis against her will, ready for the entire watching police force to laugh and/or vomit in disgust themselves. This was a pretty common situation for trans characters in media in the 90s; they existed, but to be ridiculed or displayed as objects of disgust and horror. I felt uncomfortable about my gender assigned at birth, but I didn't want to admit to the world I was that punchline. I didn't want to admit to myself that I was that punchline. As a result, I leaned into my new deep voice and facial hair. I hated them, but they kept me safe from having to answer tough questions about myself.

Every day, I had to choose between acknowledging the deep discomfort I was feeling, or hiding it and suffering alone. For years, I chose suffering. The more I leant into trying to hide it, the more it hurt. The more it hurt, the more I knew this was a real thing I was experiencing, and that it was killing me to ignore.

When it came to the exacerbation of my autism symptoms, I found that my symptoms got worse at around the same time, but for very different reasons. I reached the point in schooling where we began to prepare for GCSE exams, which brought with it a series of additional structural challenges. When kids reach their mid-teens in UK education, they start to prepare for their GCSE exams, a big part of which is picking subjects to study and subjects to drop. As a result of the broadening of the curriculum, as well as a switched focus to ability-based groupings, the education system becomes a lot less rigidly structured. Rather than having the same classes, on the same days, every single week, many schools like my own switch to an alternating two-week rota in order to fit in the expanded list of classes. One Monday might have maths in the morning, the next Monday starts with cookery. This switch from a predictable, static rota to one that kept changing hugely distressed me, because it took away my ability to confidently know something about how my day would play out based solely on what day of the week it was. I would no longer automatically pair one data point with a predictable series of events, and that made it not only more difficult for me to remain organised, but also to remain calm while navigating my days. The number of times I completely forgot to complete homework or to bring it into a lesson was honestly ridiculous, and I can't blame people for pinning it on laziness or a lack of effort on my part to be organised. I didn't have the words to explain that it was the school that had ripped routine and structure from me, and that it was their changes to my routine making it hard for me to keep on top of my work.

On top of this, the change to a GCSE curriculum-based routine also meant that I no longer had the stability of the same people in every class I attended. Up until GCSEs began, every year of my education, I had all my classes with the same thirty people: thirty students with whom I went through Reception up to Year 6, thirty new students Years 7 to 9, then all of a sudden every lesson was a different group of people, with seating plans based on who gets to which room from the previous class first. Every class it's different spaces, different people, often different rooms. Every class was a fresh state of new situations to encounter.

Then, there's the homework schedule, which steps up at

GCSE level. There's no firm rhyme or reason to when homework is or is not given, nor when it is due in. Some days no classes will assign homework, and other days three different classes will. Some days no homework is due, some days several pieces are. Some homework is due in the next instance of the class; other homework isn't due until a week and a half later. The fact that there was no set homework pattern made not only remembering to do it and hand it in difficult, but also caused distress around the lack of routine outside of school. Until the uptick in homework, my free time was entirely my own, and I could plan how to spend it to whatever obsessive degree I wanted. I could always plan in advance my time after school, and that was a refuge from the unpredictability of life. However, once homework was thrown in as a randomised element, I became unable to plan how much free time I would have outside of school, what work if any I would have to do and how long it would take me to complete.

With both my in-school and at-home routines shaken up, I lost the constants that had allowed me to keep my brain under control and my symptoms just got more and more difficult to avoid. It's easier to navigate an ocean of overwhelming sensory information when there are predictable constants you can aim for and know will be where they should be. Without that, it becomes like trying to stumble your way through a place you've never been, drowned in visual and audio static.

On top of this, one of my key autism relaxation methods fell apart around this age: due to my feelings of dysphoria, I stopped feeling comfortable swimming. Because my body was changing in ways I was deeply uncomfortable with, I found over time that I was less and less comfortable displaying my body when swimming, and as such missed out on the autism relaxation benefits of a nice swim. Some days I would be fine, others I'd be unable to stand the idea of people seeing my body.

I love swimming: the constant pressure of the water, the ability to move freely and the muted quiet when you're submerged under the water. Growing up, swimming was one of my favourite things to do when I was stressed or anxious. It made me feel calm and safe and allowed me momentary respite from sensory issues. The last time I swam was around age 17, and I didn't swim again until I was in my mid- to late 20s, after I'd had lower surgery to turn my penis into a vagina. Swimming was the biggest thing I missed during that decade of dysphoria, and my first swimming trip as an adult I just swam by myself for four hours without getting out of the pool. I'd missed it so dearly, but dysphoria had kept me from engaging in such a key autism management tool.

The problem I think for me was that all of these issues hit me at the same time, and that combination ultimately made me feel like my whole world was falling apart around me. I'd known my routine, and I knew I could keep how I felt under wraps. Suddenly my world was chaotic, changing, uncertain and unpredictable, with me at the centre of it unable to ignore how much I disliked who I was. I'd struggled before this with socialising, but at this point it just got harder and harder. Not only was I too trusting, unable to read people properly, bad at understanding social cues and non-literal meanings, but on top of that I was leaning hard into a presentation and personality I did not feel comfortable with, trying to avoid admitting I was a comedy punchline incarnate.

This was at the same time as my peers started to move towards more complex social dynamics. My teenage peers were starting to push for independence, choose their own friends based not solely on proximity, push social boundaries, engage with more intricate social politics and make use of more unspoken rules regarding how socialisation was meant to occur. The step up in my peers' social skills not only caused me to feel more isolated, but also became a point of ridicule, where my lack of ability was more easily picked up. I was more easily misled, mocked or confused than my peers, which encouraged them to make a point of making fun of me specifically for being different. This just hit home: I didn't fit in.

The more stressed I became, the less I slept. The less I slept, the more exhausted I became, the more exhausted I became, the more I started to stim and isolate myself and feel overwhelmed. The more I struggled, the more I was bullied. The more I was bullied, the more afraid I became to face my own discomfort.

The more these piled up, the more I wanted nothing more than to get out of my own head.

It was around this time that being LGBT and on the autism spectrum began to have enough of a visible effect on my life that my parents first started to suspect something was going on. I didn't tell them I was a lesbian trans woman with autism, because the whole point was that while I was struggling with symptoms, I didn't yet know what was causing them. That was partly thanks to not knowing that I fit certain diagnostic criteria. Part of it was due to worrying that maybe everyone felt this way and was just better at hiding it. Part of it was down to me not being ready to face and accept that this was who I was, and nothing would change that fact.

As a devout Christian at the time, I prayed for years to be fixed or cured. I prayed every night that one day I would wake to a quiet world, nothing overwhelming, with my mind and body in sync. I prayed to be normal, to be comfortable, to be someone who I didn't hate myself for being. I prayed to get out of a head so messed up I often thought death would be preferable to an existence this separated from the world, not knowing the what or why.

I prayed to have a brain that didn't want to kill itself...

It depends on how you look at things, whether or not my prayers were answered. I prayed to not be trans or have autism, and neither of those prayers were answered, but I suppose the prayers to be happy in my own head were eventually answered in a roundabout way.

That time in my life was perhaps the darkest I have ever lived through. I very persistently had thoughts of suicide, and the idea of ever understanding what was wrong with me seemed an impossible dream. I attempted to commit suicide three times as a teenager; once by drowning myself in the ocean, once by swallowing pills and once by suffocation. I failed to insulate the space properly to suffocate; my body forced me to the surface for air when trying to drown. The morning after I overdosed on pills, I woke up and took myself to A&E (ER), where I was given medication to make me throw up, and to block the absorption of some of what I took.

So much of what society told me about being gay, trans or having autism painted a terrible picture of my future. I was going to be a laughing stock, an ostracised obsessive loner who couldn't be trusted. I would be attacked for who I was. I would always have these issues; these problems were all inherent and would never go away. I had nothing in the way of positive autistic, gay or trans role models in my life at the time, and I felt as if acknowledging any of those aspects of myself to be true was tantamount to giving in and accepting that my life was going to be bad no matter what I did.

On top of this, having autism made it harder for me to realise my gender dysphoria was something that other people experienced, due to the struggles I had reading and connecting with other people. I didn't cotton on for a long time to the fact that other people had a different relationship to gender than me, and the fact that I was more like the women in my life than the men. Without a stable social network, I didn't have a comparison framework from which to discover that how I felt was abnormal. Ultimately, most of the early trans people I met, I met due to us both having autism. I met them through autism, and only later discovered their trans status. I felt like I understood those people on some inherent level, and as it turns out there was a ruddy good reason.

When things started to pick up
So far, this chapter has been a bit doom and gloom, but it's actually not all negatives. Some truly lovely people came into

my life around this time, due to the discovery that we shared some areas of interest. That's right, we're returning to areas of specialist interest as social coping tools.

I talked earlier in this book about how in the early years of my education, I made use of an obsessive interest in Pokémon to socialise, using the franchise as a social safety net topic. While Pokémon, and similar Japanese cartoons, sort of went out of style with my peers as they started to feel too mature for anything aimed at kids, the idea of an interest in anime being a cool thing came somewhat full circle in my teenage years. I'd kept obsessively following Pokémon through the years, but also other anime programs like DeathNote, DragonBall Z and Naruto. I found other people with those same interests, and we started to build friendships based around the fact we shared an obsessive encyclopedic knowledge of these topics.

One example of this is that when I was around 16 years old, I brought into school a notebook themed around the show DeathNote, whose central plot hinges on a magical notebook. One of the first long-term friends I made as an adult, I made thanks to that notebook. I was running the lighting for a school disco, and a woman named Emma saw the notebook and asked me about my interest in the show. There was enough discussion room there for me to safely and comfortably talk to her for a couple of hours, and she even wanted to talk more afterwards. I knew that she was into anime, and as such I used anime as a safety topic. Any time I ran short of things to say, or wasn't sure how best to continue a conversation, I would go back to that safety topic and feel comfortable and relaxed socially. In hindsight, as sweet as that story is when told this way, it could so easily have turned out terribly and caused me a lot of problems. The notebook in the show causes people to die if their names are written down, and it would not have taken much for someone to have spun that as a warning sign that I was dangerous to my peers or something. It was a lovely exchange, that as an adult I am just thankful didn't go horribly wrong.

The same happened with music. I found out that I shared an obsessive interest in bands like My Chemical Romance with some of my teenage peers, which made it easier to meet new people. I made friends with one of my first ever non-school based friends because I was working a Saturday job in a sweet shop while wearing a My Chemical Romance t-shirt. She came up and asked me about my interest in the band, I wowed her with my knowledge of facts and figures about them and we became friends. As much as I struggled socially, I always had that band as a safety topic, something to bond over and something to listen to in awkward silences to help share an experience. If I found myself unsure how to continue a conversation, I could just start playing a My Chemical Romance song on my phone, and those friends would enjoy my company for a time. That was something I could rely on.

Lastly, my obsessive interest in video games helped me to make friends. I spent so much time by myself playing games, reading about games and listening to people talk about games, that I became the go to person in my friendship group to answer questions about what was coming out and when, what was worth playing and how to get through games. That particular obsessive interest ended up being the catalyst for my eventual career path. In my twenties I ended up getting a career as a professional video game critic, a full-time paid job that kept a roof over my head and is still my primary job today. It was one of the first times in my life that I realised an obsessive level of interest in and knowledge of a subject might not be a bad thing. Once you hit your teenage years, and people start to not only pick their own interests, but more heavily invest their sense of identity in those interests, it's easier to rely on one topic to maintain a friendship for a number of years. As long as their interest in that topic doesn't pass, it's enough to avoid being alone. I found that, during my teen years, women were more open to being friends with me, so long as we shared obsessive interests. I wasn't welcome in same-gender events, like sleepovers, but I was at least welcome socially in group situations, and that helped a lot. I was the non-threatening male friend who just loooooved to squeal about shared interests, and that was enough for me to start making my first proper friends. Sure, I was leaning heavily on safety topics as a crutch, but it was real notable steps of progress.

The downside to this increase in friendships was that I ended up falling into many of the same traps I had fallen into as a child, but without requiring the same level of manipulation or coercion to end up there. Where as a child people like Daniel had manipulated me by threatening actively to abandon me if I went against them, in my teen years I ultimately put that pressure on myself, because that was the only childhood model I really had upon which to base friendships. The last time I'd had people willing to stick around me in life, it had been made clear I had to go along with things I was uncomfortable with, or the result would be threats of social isolation. I knew to shut up, fit in, do what everyone else did, or as I saw it my friendships would fall apart. The idea of a friendship where disagreement or saying no to someone was not a cardinal sin had simply not occurred to me. As a result, based on observation of social models rather than any active pressure in the moment, I went into a lot of my teenage friendships fearing a threat of isolation that was never actually made. This caused me to start doing something I had never previously done: breaking rules of my own volition. I lied to my parents about where I was going in order to not miss events I knew I shouldn't be attending, I skipped classes to spend time with those friends, I went underage drinking and I did a number of things that were in hindsight dangerous or risky behaviours.

As a teenager, I would tell my parents I was going for a sleepover at the house of a friend from church, before hopping a fence and sneaking past security to get underage drunk on a section of beach my friends knew was never patrolled. I would skip classes in order to sit and socialise with friends, because I feared missing some important situation that would cause the group's dynamic to change, or a vital in-joke being created while I was absent. I would go out into town at lunch rather than do my homework, again out of fear that my newfound social circle would abandon me. Past experience told me that if I didn't do everything I was expected to, I would return to isolation, and that scared me even more than the consequences of my choices.

I also did things that, while not morally wrong, felt wrong to me on a personal comfort level. I lost my voluntary virginity – something that I wasn't comfortable doing while presenting male, not least because of some of the parts of my body that involved – because I believed doing so was something that would help me to establish some sense of internal or external validity as masculine. It didn't work, but these were the kind of things I did to try to convince myself that I could be like my peers, that I could be who the world expected me to be. I thought that if I had penetrative sex, using my penis, I would maybe feel more like a man, or that my peers would see me more as deserving of the masculinity I was meant to embody by circumstance of birth. Ultimately, it just made me feel weird. That wasn't the side of that equation I felt I was meant to be on.

During these years, I spent a lot of time ignoring societal boundaries, ignoring my own personal boundaries and ignoring who I wanted to be, in the pursuit of maintaining friendships I saw as under attack from the threats of a decade prior. I can see a decade after these events that I probably didn't need to do any of that, but it was the messed up view of social interactions I had been left holding. I used past results as an indicator of future outcomes, and acted accordingly. This whole model was sort of how I got through these years, using past data to extrapolate future outcomes. Basically, I created social flow charts. Not hypothetical ones in my mind, but real literal physical ones.

I would sit in classes making conversational scripts, plotting out template conversations which would help me meet new people, planning out my evenings minute by minute, and slotting in variable branches in conversations for what I would do if I needed to slot in a safety topic. Any time a conversation went in a direction I had not prepared for, I would return to the flow chart and remake it, adding in new branches of how to respond. I tried to treat people and social situations as mathematical equations with set solutions, where I could plug in the data and know a successful result. It wasn't healthy, but it was a way to survive. It was a way to keep going and manage tough unknown situations.

My teen years were a mess of uncertainty, confusion, chaos and self-dislike. I was making friends, but because of past abuse, I was assuming I had to be someone I was not to maintain them. I was using time I should have used for schoolwork plotting out social flow charts. I was doing things that were morally wrong, or that I was uncomfortable doing, just because I thought it would help me fit in, be more comfortable or avoid further isolation. I was being bullied for who I was, running from who I was and generally unaware of who I was. Those years were a mess, full of many choices and decisions I am ultimately not proud of: choices and decisions that almost cost me my family's support, and almost sent my life down a dangerous path. I love some of the people I met, but I can't love who I was.

Using emo aesthetics to test the waters

My mid- to late teen years occurred in the mid- to late 2000s, and as a depressed hormonal teenager living through those years, I was lucky to find an aesthetic subculture to fall into that allowed me some scope to experiment with more feminine presentation without being assumed to be not male. I spent several years dressing like the poster child for the mid-2000s emo subculture. For any of you reading this book who are not 'the right age at the right time', the stereotypical image of a mid-2000s emo is a skinny teenager with straight black hair swept across one half of their face, lots of red and black clothing, some Converse shoes, wristbands and lots of spikes, studs or checkered fingerless gloves. Imagine goths, if they were a little more feminine in appearance, and their clothing was tighter fitting.

In terms of associated personality traits, people who considered themselves emo were basically kids with depression but who lacked the emotional vocabulary required to explain to someone that they were constantly sad for no reason and maybe they needed some actual medical help to sort that out. It was the support group culture for kids who due to trauma needed to mature too soon, and they sort of lacked the healthy coping mechanisms to deal with the onset of depression when their peers around them were maturing in healthier ways. Emo fashion aesthetics identified to others that you were likely someone with baggage, but that you understood what it was like to have that specific flavour of depression, and as such might be someone relatable. It was a way to find others who were struggling and to feel a little less alone.

With that preamble about emos out of the way, the reason I sort of fell into that subculture during the years things were getting tougher for me was primarily the somewhat gender-flexible aspects that embodied the emo style of dress. Everyone was encouraged to grow their hair long and use it to cover up some of their face, which appealed to me as someone looking to grow their hair long without being accused of not being male as a result, and as someone who struggled with their appearance and liked the idea of having less of their facial structure on show. On top of that, it was a fashion style where people, regardless of gender, tended to wear the same colours of clothing, the same types of jeans and shoes, the same types of accessories, hoodies and even accessories like bracelets. It was a fashion style where it was commonly joked guys would buy their jeans from the women's section of stores leaving them with flat crotch appearances, and where being more visibly emotional than your peers was seen as a positive, not a failure of masculinity. It was one of the few social cliques of the era where crying, as someone perceived male, was not a reason to invalidate someone. It certainly wasn't free of its own share of controversy. I remember well one night at a party at my aunt's home where my mother asked if I was part of a suicide cult, because she had read a news story where *The Sun* had presented the subculture as being about scoring points via self-harm and suicide attempts, and that the band My Chemical Romance's album The Black Parade was a call to kill oneself to impress the band, which makes me laugh today looking at the context of the album's themes of 'not [being] afraid to keep on living'. Still, regardless of the way it was perceived by older generations, it gave me space to grow my hair out, cry when I needed to, dress very similarly to my female friends, experiment with more traditionally feminine clothing and accessories and do so without having my status as male questioned.

CHAPTER 4

Coming Out of the Closet

Between the ages of 16 and 17, while I wasn't yet ready to seriously come out as trans, I experimented more than once with gendered presentation, in ways that in hindsight I honestly find a little bit hilarious. I'm going to tell you some stories, and these are all of things that occurred before I came out as trans. They were all just silly joke goofs, definitely not anything serious I wanted to explore. Of course not, that would be ridiculous.

At age 17, I had a couple of friends I was attending college with, one of whom was at the time female presenting. Over lunch, they suggested I'd look really cute in one of their tops, and we joked back and forth that I should wear some of their clothes and come along to their art classroom for lunch, under the guise that I was a new student at the school. The idea was to see how long I could get away with pretending to be female, and if anyone would notice or say anything. When asked my name, I told them it was Laura, and I spent the rest of that lunch period presenting as female. Such a funny goof. All guys do this at some point, don't they? All assigned male at birth people at some point pick a female name and pass themselves off as female without any kind of joke reveal at the end.

A couple of months later, I was preparing to attend an anime convention with some friends, and we were trying to pick out our costumes. We had been watching as a group a show called Ouran High School Host Club, about a group of students in a Japanese school. One of the characters has a parent who is presented as being a trans woman. They're referred to as being the character's dad, but are very clearly femme presenting and have a preference for female pronouns. I offered to, once again as a total joke, cosplay as the character's 'dad', a very minor character, but one that would just about make sense if I stayed with the group. I went and purchased a skirt, blouse and cardigan combination that in hindsight made me look like I had dressed out of a far older woman's wardrobe. I remember getting changed into the outfit in a friend's bathroom with great difficulty, and being loaned a bra to stuff to complete the outfit. It didn't suit me at all, but I really loved it as a totally joke outfit that was definitely not to be taken seriously.

At that same event, during one evening in a hotel, all of the women I had travelled with were doing their makeup ready for an evening out and I once again joked that it would be oh so funny if they did my hair and makeup too, just to see how I looked. They proceeded to spend around an hour making me up; all the while I laughed about how silly and ridiculous it was.

I also remember, in that same sort of time frame, starting an account in the online game World of Warcraft under a female name, with the expectation that if anyone realised I was assigned male at birth, I would play it all off as a big joke.

All of these experiences were during a few years where, if asked, I would have vehemently denied being transgender. I was terrified of the implications of transition, and of a change that drastic to my own sense of self-image and identity. There were days I went to sixth form with a stuffed bra under my biking jacket, hoping it would go unnoticed under the bulk of the top layer. I continually told myself that I was attracted to women, so I wasn't gay, and so there was no aspect of my identity I needed to examine. I didn't quite realise that gender and sexuality could be separated, and that my interest in women didn't preclude me from being a woman myself.

What ultimately convinced me to come out as transgender, at age 17, was a friend from college named Jess, who had noticed the frequency of my jokes about gender and subtly recommended that I watch an anime series titled *Wandering Son*. The show itself is fairly short, at 12 episodes, and focuses on a pair of children who are both uncomfortable with their birth assigned gender, one assigned male at birth and one assigned female, as they help each other explore the world of transition and work out how they can be comfortable with themselves. While it was not the first time I had seen transgender people acknowledged in media, it was the first time I saw them humanised, presented as real people and made relatable to myself. They were just normal people who happened to feel at odds with their assigned at birth gender, and decided they'd be happier if they presented themselves differently to the world, were addressed by new pronouns, but just kept living their lives. It was a story that involved some sneaking around, some clashes with the world, but ultimately they were happier for acknowledging how they felt about themselves and for having experienced a different role in life. It was a tasteful and humanising story that rang so many bells for me, written in a way that sounded so familiar to all those private thoughts I had spent years internalising. I had never told anyone how I felt, and suddenly this show just understood everything I had ever left unsaid.

I finished watching the show and just stared silently at a blank wall for several hours, crying. I spoke to the friend who recommended it to me a few days later, and she admitted that she'd had her suspicions and thought I might benefit from seeing it. I ended up that night messaging a very close friend, incredibly emotionally overwhelmed and not sure how to verbalise how I felt. I eventually spluttered out that I thought I might feel more comfortable living as a woman, and she jumped on the opportunity to offer me advice. I was incredibly lucky in hindsight; it turns out the friend I had just come out to knew a transgender man, someone assigned female at birth but living as male, and as such had some knowledge of therapists I could talk to, things I could try at home and how I could go about progressing things if those early steps proved positive.

Over the years that followed, I experimented with gendered presentation quietly, without making any big solid announcements about myself. I experimented with using female names to refer to myself, seeing if any of them felt like they fit.

I went and sheepishly bought my first outfits, totally unsure of my clothing size, by ordering online and pretending I was just picking them up for someone else. I used to stand in the bathroom of my parent's home, completely without their knowledge, taking photos of myself in dresses, seeing what I felt like when I saw myself.

I came out to a small group of friends around age 18, who were all surprisingly supportive. I used to leave my house presenting male, get to my friend's house, say hello and head straight to her bathroom to change my clothes. They were really good about giving me a safe space to try out female presentation and just find out in a risk-free environment what it was like to be seen, referred to and treated as Laura. They even bought me a selection of scarves as a gift, so I could more easily hide my huge Adam's apple. It didn't take me long at all to work out that this was what I needed; that this was the route to relieving some of the dysphoria I had spent years struggling with. I felt I had to talk to a professional, so I took some earlier advice and started seeing a therapist who specialises in talking to people about gender dysphoria. I spent a few months attending the therapy sessions in total secret. I lied to work and told them I had a regular volunteer appointment to keep each week, so I could get the time off work. I would finish work presenting male, drive over to the counselling centre and get changed into different clothes in the bathroom before going into appointments as Laura. It took a few months of talking, but over time over time became apparent that yes, transitioning did seem like the best way forward for me, and that was going to inevitably mean letting people in all areas of my life know, which was terrifying.

I told my mother I thought I might be trans in a lengthy and overly apologetic email, which she didn't quite know how to respond to. From her perspective, my transition had popped up out of nowhere, with no prior warning signs. She was convinced I had been brainwashed into transitioning, and agreed to meet my counsellor for a joint meeting with me, primarily to meet the person she felt had brainwashed her child into transitioning. My mother describes her first meeting with me presenting as Laura as very difficult for her, due in no small part to her inability to see me as anything but her very traditionally masculine son in a dress. For a while she knew but did not talk to my father, which she found very difficult. She told me years later that she went through a period of mourning, feeling like her child had died, and that she was left with a stranger she did not know. It put a lot of strain on her, and on our relationship as parent and child. Why the assumption I was brainwashed? Because of autism infantilisation.

Before we talk more about my journey coming out as transgender, we have to rewind a little bit to something else that went on at around the same point in my life: my diagnosis of Asperger's. By the time my mother attended that appointment and met me as Laura for the first time, I had already been diagnosed with Asperger's, which was part of the reason she was so worried about me. She was not aware of any statistical link between autism and gender dysphoria, and in her eyes I was a vulnerable young person with an autism spectrum condition who was being manipulated into transition because I was easily swayed, or lacking in ability to assess my feelings on the matter properly for myself. This is depressingly common: an adult's assumption that having an autism spectrum condition means you're incapable of proper self-understanding, or that you're susceptible to being manipulated into believing things about yourself that you did not previously. You're not trusted as being of sound mind to make choices about your own life, out of fear you've been manipulated.

Speaking to my mother years later, now she has somewhat settled down and got used to me going by Laura and female pronouns, she told me that her biggest fear, and the primary reason she agreed to attend that first joint session together, was that, as a youth with Asperger's, my therapist was influencing me into believing that I was trans. She feared it was some kind of brainwashing that my gullible mind could not resist the allure of, rather than believing my own account of what I was experiencing.

I also faced this same issue with doctors when trying to access medical support through the NHS. I would have general practitioners, mental health doctors and gender specialists alike raise an eyebrow when I acknowledged my Asperger's diagnosis, and then proceed to take plenty of extra time asking me lengthy questions about how my autism symptoms manifested, to ensure I was of sound enough mind to make permanent choices about my body. Apart from the obvious infantilisation of people with conditions like Asperger's on display there, I always just explained it as being like the decision to get a tattoo. I am an adult, over the age of 18, who has been deemed sober and mentally sound, and as such I have every right to permanently inject colours into my skin that may never go away. Why should I not be trusted to take slow-acting meds that are somewhat easier to reverse? Still, the fact I had to fight to be believed that I was mentally sound enough to make that choice says a lot about misunderstandings about autism spectrum conditions, but highlights that to assert that transition is unique in the permanent nature of its change to the body is completely inaccurate.

So, let's tell the story of my Asperger's diagnosis. When I was around 16 to 17 my mother began to notice me exhibiting a number of unusual behaviours and encouraged me to seek an appointment with the youth mental health service for counselling. She wasn't pushing for me to attend specifically because of suspicions of an autism spectrum condition; that idea didn't come up until my counsellor brought it up quite some way into our sessions. My mother just knew there was something odd, different, unusual and strange about some of my behaviours. My unusual behaviours were starting to be a problem, and beginning to inconvenience her life as much as mine. Initially, sessions focused more generally on my life, my oddities, stress and unusual methods of stress management. I talked about family issues, I talked about school and eventually I started to talk about feeling overwhelmed by changes to routine. My counsellor recognised that I was engaging in stimming when stressed in sessions, something I at the time didn't know existed, and she recommended I seek an assessment for Asperger's. I brought the suggestion up to my mother, who after reading up on the condition, quickly got on board with the idea, as it seemed to explain a lot of the odd quirks I had spent most of my life exhibiting. I went through the assessment, and was diagnosed with Asperger's a week before I turned 18. The result of this was that I was diagnosed and then with no further support, I was dropped from my counsellor and left to understand the diagnosis myself. I had become too old for the youth mental health service, so I was instantly dropped from support.

My mother took to the diagnosis like a duck to water; she very quickly noted that many of my long held behavioural quirks now made sense, and was quick to help me find support groups and materials to learn how to better cope.

My stepfather on the other hand was a lot more wary of my diagnosis. He's considerably older than my mother, and was born in a generation where mental health support was far less widely recognised as legitimate. As a result, he had some scepticism in the early months after my diagnosis. He was also considerably less open than my mother to LGBT topics, hence my having not come out to him as trans yet. The result of this is a story about how my autism symptoms, as well as my hidden trans status, both exploded in a very angry and emotional argument one day after dinner.

The fight when I came out to Dad

In the months after getting diagnosed with Asperger's, my life had begun to change considerably. On the one hand, putting a name to my condition allowed me to research coping mechanisms and discover formally that stimming was a thing that existed. As a result of knowing my odd tics were a recognised thing, and something that genuinely served a purpose in helping me manage my symptoms, I began to stim more visibly, no longer forcing the same level of secrecy on actions designed to help me stay calm and concentrated.

However, at the same time, I was hiding a pretty big secret with regards to my trans status. I could see knowing I was trans and worrying about me transitioning, but not being able to share that with anyone around her was putting a toll on my mother, which was distressing for me to see. I was trying to live two simultaneous lives by this point: my social life with friends as Laura, but my home and work lives under a male name and pronouns. I would have to hide specifics of where I had been, I couldn't invite friends to my house and any time I left the house I had to smuggle out clothing hoping nobody would ask what I was carrying so secretively. I couldn't share any pictures of the time I spent with my friends. I couldn't show my family the creative projects I was working on, as they were under the name Laura. As a result of this exhausting double life I was trying to live, I found my anxiety was considerably worse, and I ended up experiencing even more trouble keeping myself emotionally in check. This was paired with me moving to sixth form, where there was even less routine and structure than GCSE education, and in spite of better understanding of my condition and coping mechanisms, my visible autism traits were becoming at times more obvious and extreme.

One night I was trying to help wash up after dinner but was struggling due to some oversensitivity to the smells involved, and I asked to be excused. My stepdad said no, I had to stay and help, which I tried to do, taking breaks during the process to stim. Dad did not respond well to this. He started shouting about how I had really been playing up my autism symptoms since I received a diagnosis, and was clearly just acting up for attention, and to get out of doing things I didn't want to do. I didn't respond. I just spent a few seconds hugging myself and rocking, then tried to get back to the chore at hand. He kept getting louder, telling me I needed to just stop doing the stimming and stop acting like autism was a real issue in my life, telling me the need to stim was something I had invented for my own convenience. I continued to become more anxious, trying to stim to deal with the noise and the allegations and the smells. He continued to insist I was stimming just to get him to stop telling me truths I didn't want to hear.

I felt trapped, cornered and overwhelmed, a feeling that grew to a full meltdown, where I took myself to one side and started hitting at my own head. I felt like my head was full of static, it was in my eyes and ears and brain and mouth and it was overwhelming me, like a swarm of angry bees or an untuned TV, and I just didn't know how else to get myself back into a focused state. Hitting myself was very loud sensory information, which I knew when to expect. I could focus on the hitting and get through the static and back to the room. It's not healthy, but it's what I did.

This encouraged Dad to just shout louder about how I was

making everything up. Mum chimed in, stating that I was dealing with more than just the autism, and if he only knew he might have some empathy. Dad started shouting that if there was something else in my life, I should explain it now.

And that's how I came out as trans to my dad. I was in mid-autism meltdown, hitting my head, crying and overwhelmed, and I sort of scream shouted at him that I felt uncomfortable in my body and wanted to live as female. Things calmed down a little from there. There were reassurances. I was given some space to breathe in silence until I felt better. I gave a little explanation and then went to bed. It wasn't ideal, but it was out in the open at least.

From here, things got rough for a while. I was still living at home, but the lack of structure created by moving from GCSE education to A levels was taking its toll on my mental health. I reached a point where I was having to be self-motivated, in an incredibly fluid routine environment, and things didn't go well as a result. Where I had been a very successful student at GCSE level, I failed my A level exams twice in a row at two different schools, due largely to having too much openness and too little structure in my routine. There were no longer any formal seating plans, I might have multiple teachers for the same subject, I bounced between different start and finish times every day and was entirely responsible for finding a way to create a stable structure out of things. After I failed my exams for the second time in a row, I panicked. My entire life plan up to that point had been school, then A levels, then to go off to university. I had planned my life around this traditional education to employment pathway, and without that I honestly had no idea what I was meant to do with my life. The world was completely wide open, with no predefined path, and no planned options, and I had no clue how to respond.

I think the way I ultimately responded says a lot about where my life was at that point. I kept going to sixth form, in spite of no longer being enrolled there as a student. I didn't tell my friends I had failed to get accepted to my second year, I didn't tell my parents; I just went to the school cafe which was open all day and the main social area, socialised for a few hours and then went home. I couldn't work out how to handle the idea that I had no remaining direction for my life, and I was terrified of the consequences of admitting to my parents that I had failed my exams a second time. In hindsight, it's obvious I could have, and should have, just talked to my parents and asked for their help and support to make a new plan for the future. I didn't, not because they'd ever done anything to make me feel I couldn't safely talk to them, but because I felt like everything I was doing in my life was making me a failure without a future. Having been treated as one of the bright kids at school, I thought the fact that I was suddenly failing would be put down to laziness, and didn't know how to explain the factors causing me problems. I was afraid that they would see me as having given up on life, as having decided that post-autism diagnosis I no longer had to try and could just laze through life, and was afraid that they would be just as afraid as I was about my uncertain future. I pretended to keep going to college for several months, before eventually being caught out by my mother. She contacted the school to check in on my attendance statistics, learned I was no longer a student, and I had probably the most difficult day of my life as a result. I came home filled with guilt, unsure how to explain to my mother why I had done what I had done, failed to give any reasonable explanations, and went to bed without dinner to cry myself to sleep.

The months that followed involved invasions of privacy, which limited my ability to explore my gender identity safely at home, and robbed me of the feeling of comfort and security that four solid predictable walls provided me as someone with an autism spectrum disorder. I was subjected to rules, stipulations and slowly moving goalposts regarding when and how my transition would eventually be supported. I was a depressed young adult whose actions had led to them having no privacy, no plans for the future, no ability to explore who they were and no idea how they were ever going to get to a place in life where they would be happy about who they were. You could argue it was my own fault, but it was a very rough time in my life. I remember that time in very vague terms. I remember a depressed haze, a muddle of days and weeks filled with sadness, loss, confusion and guilt. I remember having no clue who I would be a few years down the line, or if I would even still be here. Probably the worst part of it all was that I knew I was depressed, but I was afraid to get help, for fear it would stop me being able to get help transitioning.

Things did eventually start to pull back together. I got a job at a budget supermarket, I started making enough money to pay rent to my parents, I was able to start getting some privacy back into my life and, after a considerable amount of time, I was able to start presenting as female here and there at home.

My parents were not happy with me spending most of my time alone in my room after work; they wanted me to contribute to housework and socialise more, but I honestly just wanted space to talk to friends online who fully accepted me as Laura, and were willing to let me just explore who I was going to be going forwards. I ultimately moved out of my parents' home, into a tiny one-bedroom flat above a pub with my girlfriend, where I was able to present full time as female without any worry of being misgendered or dead named. I found it tough, but my life was becoming my own, and I was starting to find the freedom to work out who I was all over from scratch, on my own terms.

Coming out at work didn't go very smoothly. On paper, my workplace appeared reasonably supportive. When I brought up the topic of transition with my boss, and explained to him that all those days I had to leave work early were for therapy about gender, he was understanding enough to get that he had to do things right and couldn't prevent me transitioning. I took a week away from work, was given a new female uniform and name tag, and came back to work as Laura. Employees were generally quite good about things, for a few months, until things went wrong. In terms of employee response, a few staff members got funny about me using the women's bathroom, slip ups with my name and gender became more common, I walked in more than once on transphobic discussions about me and I found out that at least one staff member had requested not to be put on shifts with me following my transition. I ended up leaving the job within a few months of transition, but thankfully had a backup job already lined up. During my time working at the supermarket, I had been spending most of my free time writing unpaid articles about video games on the internet. It started as a way to pass the time and keep myself engaged at work. I had always enjoyed talking about video games with my peers, and I was aware that there were people on the internet who did it as a full-time job. I wasn't sure how to make the leap from unpaid to paid work, but I knew that a portfolio of free work was a place to start. I came up with ideas in a notebook while at work, wrote them when I came home at night and repeated this every day for quite some time. When I left the supermarket job, I took a risk. I had a few months' savings and I had a bit of an audience online, so I took one month to try to make enough money to survive purely by writing about games. It was a career I had only ever done under a female name; I'd been writing as Laura from day one, and in that first month I had made just enough money to scrape by and survive. From then on, I was only ever Laura. I was working a dream job, I was living full time as Laura, I was in a phase of my life where people only knew me as Laura, and that was sort of when I feel my life truly began.

I was Laura. I was out in the world, I had a career goal to build and work through. My life was my own, I could set my own predictable schedule that didn't change from one week to the next, and I could freely explore who I was and how I wanted the world to see me. This was when I started to finally build a life that worked for me, as a woman and as an adult living with autism.

CHAPTER 5

Depression and Addiction

During this same turbulent few years of my life, while I was just starting to go through the NHS for gender dysphoria treatment, there were regular horror stories about people being refused trans treatments if they were depressed. I know plenty of cis people who have depression; depression isn't some issue that's inextricably tied to being trans, making it impossible to treat dysphoria until generalised depression is gone. There's no real reason that being depressed should stop the NHS from treating your dysphoria, but I saw it happen time and time again.

NHS waiting list times in the UK when I started trying to seek dysphoria treatment were several years long, and they've only got worse over time. Gender dysphoria is one of the few mental health areas currently where waiting lists to even get seen by someone, let alone receive any support or treatment, are commonly longer than two years, and if you're still mid-puberty when you start that waiting list, time is ticking. Every month spent waiting for treatment is another month of changes your body has made that you'll have to work to fight back against. Hearing that trans people who reported depression were made to get that sorted first, then had to join a waiting list for treatment at the bottom ensured I never got treatment for my depression. I denied it existed to doctors because I was afraid of having to live through potentially two or more extra years before getting the help and treatment I needed.

As a result of living for several years with untreated depression, I initially struggled severely with suicidal urges, and suicide attempts that thankfully failed. However, I found a different source of support instead, one that didn't involve alerting medical professionals to my struggles. I began self-medicating my depression with addictive chemicals.

Addiction

It took me until well into my 20s to properly come to terms with the fact that I'm prone to addiction. It wasn't a sudden revelation, but a slow repeated awareness that got harder and harder to ignore. I am not necessarily physically addicted to chemicals, but I am prone to becoming addicted to short-term fixes for long-term mental health struggles.

For a long time, it was generally assumed by the medical community that if someone has autism they're considerably less likely than the general population to struggle with addiction. Many early studies into addiction and autism took place before Asperger syndrome and other similar conditions were brought under the autism umbrella, and while yes, this did provide a set of data where individuals with autism had lower rates of alcohol and substance addiction, the data failed to correctly understand the causes for that data, made incorrect assumptions based on it and had too narrow a scope of what constituted addiction. By focusing these early studies largely on the types of individuals with autism who require full-time care, the focus was on individuals who largely had less access to addictive substances like drugs, alcohol or cigarettes, and the studies read that lack of access and the resulting lack in addiction as indicative of a predisposition to finding those chemicals less addictive than the general population. It's understandable why this assumption was made, because from the outside, it would make a lot of sense within the framework of what medical professionals understood about autism as a condition. Most individuals with autism are generally rigid rule followers, and most addictive substances are forbidden, so it stood to reason that those with a brain predisposed to following rules wouldn't try, or get addicted to, forbidden substances. However, if we look at more recent studies focused on self-sufficient individuals on the autism spectrum, those capable of supporting themselves without long-term support, the results paint a very different picture. If you focus on the types of individuals with autism that are in a position to experience peer pressure, to succumb to that peer pressure out of a desire for social connection and who have access to addictive substances of their own accord, addiction rates are actually much higher than is average in the general population. One fairly recent Swedish study, which focused on people with autism who had average or above average IQ, found that those individuals experienced more than twice the statistical average rates of substance addiction.[1]

As an individual living with autism who has also struggled with substance addiction, I can attest that there are a lot of similarities between how my brain feels when experiencing substance addiction and when experiencing bouts of autism-based addiction and compulsion. Autism, similar to other mental health conditions like ADHD, can cause many, but not all, sufferers to have counter-indicative responses to specific drugs. Nobody's quite certain why it happens, or why it only affects some with the condition rather than all, but caffeine as a drug is a perfect example of something that often does the opposite of what it is meant to do for individuals with autism. As you may have guessed, I am one of the individuals with autism who find the effects of caffeine counter indicative, meaning that rather than leaving me shaky and over-energised, I find it calms and relaxes me, providing me with a mental quiet I normally do not get to experience. I can't tell you why, but drugs that are meant to leave a person brimming with energy, bouncing off the walls or rushing around often simply do not have that effect on me. I do become focused, but more as a result of relaxing, tuning out a small portion of the normally overwhelming sensory information in the world around me, and getting my brain to disconnect from the constant mental chatter that overwhelms my head. As a teenager, when I first started trying drinks with a high caffeine content, I was really

---

1   www.ncbi.nlm.nih.gov/pmc/articles/PMC5222913

caught off guard by the effect it had on me compared to my peers. It was the first time in my life I really got an opportunity to experience a mind where my autism symptoms, not that I knew initially that was what they were, got just a little more quiet.

As someone whose Asperger's causes them to have a somewhat addictive personality, I ended up finding myself pretty cripplingly addicted to caffeine for a number of years. I would drink upwards of ten cans of an energy drink a day, chugging them down like they were fruit juices. I would chug down the reserves of them that my parents had in the house for themselves, I would spend my pocket money on big 1-litre bottles, I even at times stole money from my parents to buy more caffeine drinks. I somewhat lacked the vocabulary at the time to explain to my parents that I was addicted, or quite why. It was the first taste in my life of a brain less cluttered, less full of overwhelming, uncontrollable static. It was my first experience of getting to quiet down the mind, if only for a little while, and feel a little more on top of my senses. I have cut caffeine pretty much completely out of my life at this point, mainly because my consumption levels scared people close to me, but I still as an adult find it oddly calming to consume. It's not like it makes my autism symptoms go away completely, far from it; but it does offer a little control, calm and quiet in a world that often does not grant my brain that luxury.

Addiction however has been a persistent issue in my life, even after pushing aside caffeine. It was my first substance addiction in life, but it was not my first battle with addiction ever. My earliest experience with addiction was stimming, and my battle to keep that under control in order to avoid social ridicule. With both stimming and caffeine consumption, I had things I could do to reduce some of the noise and repetitive thought loops that so often fill up my mind from day to day. While they were both useful coping mechanisms, they ultimately led to negative outcomes in my life, be it getting into trouble for taking my parents' caffeine supply when I was not supposed to or getting mocked and socially excluded by my peers. In both cases I found myself just craving relief from a brain that was incessantly filled with static, constant overwhelming bombardment, and the relief I was provided with often outweighed the negative consequences I knew would result. Trying to ignore this caused my head to shout at me like a broken record, unwilling to focus on anything else. Many of the same things could be said for my obsessive need to organise, my obsessive need to line things up, my obsessive need to plan. They were all ways to calm my mind that offered a calm and quiet that I craved. I was addicted to short-term respite from the chaos.

It shouldn't come as a huge surprise that these experiences feel so similar, as they both affect largely the same areas of the brain. Studies have shown that individuals with autism often are compelled to engage in repetitive actions by the same brain regions that cause substance addicts to crave their vices, the section of the brain that automates actions and treats them as a necessary part of daily life that can't be ignored. What is vitally important to note about these addictions is that they were all incredibly short-term solutions to a very long-term problem. I've spent my whole life living with a brain that doesn't behave like most: a brain that is never quiet and calm. Stimming and drinking caffeine both calm my brain and allow me to get by, but both only help alleviate my symptoms while they're acting on my system. If I stop stimming, or the caffeine leaves my system, I am back to square one. This is why both are so addictive; they offer a moment of respite from the chaos, and returning to that lifetime of volume and static is exhausting and distressing enough to push me to return to my addictions.

Day to day, I live with a brain that feels like it never stops or slows down. It's constantly trying to process every sense, no matter how small or unimportant, and trying to find the important information in a wave of static. It's constantly fixating on plans, making me check and recheck and write down and recheck times and locations and specifics of plans. It's constantly repeating the same phrases over and over in my head, screaming at me to focus on them. It's constantly fixating on unimportant topics, not letting me put them aside mentally and get on with what I want or need to do. It's screaming at me that foods have too many textures, or that I am reading social situations wrong or that I am a burden and should just stay away from the world. It creates barriers between me and those around me that are hard to work around, and it makes every conversation a planned out exercise in social etiquette. Living with an autism spectrum condition is exhausting, and there are no known treatments to alleviate the symptoms. There's no prescribed medication available to offer me respite. I felt like my choices were to live this way every day of my life, with no relief, or to find my own ways to quiet and calm my brain, if only for a short time.

While it's no longer an issue in my life, I also struggled with alcohol addiction in my mid- to late teen years. I would lie to my parents about where I was going, and consume large amounts of alcohol on a beach while under the legal drinking age. I found that it dulled my senses by virtue of making me notice less across the board. I just generally ran a bit slower and didn't notice so much of the sensory information around me. It wasn't that I was filtering out the unimportant information and just focusing on the important; it's that across the board I was taking in less information. I picture my brain as having three dials: one for important information, one for unimportant information and one master dial for all information. Rather than alcohol turning down just the unimportant dial, it turned down the master dial. Everything was less intense, and my brain's obsessive repetitive thoughts just slowed and lessened. On top of that, people consuming alcohol tend to act a little weird and unusual, which allowed me room to fit in a little more easily, with less of my mind dedicated to worrying that I wasn't doing the right thing for the social situation. When drinking alcohol, everyone's a little weird. When consuming alcohol, I had something to blame my weird social behaviours on, an excuse to not worry if I acted strangely. A reason to not be so judged. Much like caffeine and stimming, my addiction to alcohol centred around its nature as a short-term fix for a long-term brain state. I could get drunk and experience relief from my symptoms, but as soon as I sobered up I was back to square one, and the temptation was there to get drunk again to reclaim that sense of respite.

I kicked my addiction to alcohol at around age 20, after a day where I had to admit to a friend I had brought vodka in a water bottle to a social event taking place in the morning where it was very clear nobody else would be drinking. I was forced to face the fact that I was relying on it as a crutch to manage social situations, rather than focusing on learning sober coping techniques to manage my autism symptoms in social situations. For a time, I cut out alcohol completely, before reintroducing it to my life under very strict conditions. No drinking alcohol alone by myself, no friendships where I do not feel comfortable socialising with them while sober and no denying that I have drunk. If I break any of these self-imposed rules I know I have a problem and will act accordingly. I might drink a couple of ciders in a field with my partner on a summer's day, or share a bottle of wine every few months over some board games with friends, but recognising the addiction allowed me to get it under control.

Drugs, and why I started taking them

While I've spoken above about addiction to chemical substances that are generally not feared as addictive and are socially acceptable to dabble with, I'm now going to talk a little about my experiences with substances that are more traditionally perceived as addictive.

I have as an adult consumed MDMA, and while I unequivocally believe the experience was a net positive in my life, I have had to wrestle with questions of addiction regarding the drug. MDMA, typically taken as a recreational party drug, is illegal in many countries in the world, including my own. While its primary use recreationally is to flood the brain with feelgood chemicals and create feelings of increased openness and empathy, clinical trials in the US suggest that it activates many of the same areas of the brain that function in non-standard ways in individuals with autism. From a brief appraisal, it's easy to see how a drug that induces feelings of positive empathy might be beneficial to individuals on the autism spectrum in a dry, abstract sense. For me, it was a world-changing experience, not just during the trip itself but for months afterwards. The biggest thing I immediately noticed upon reaching the high brought on by a recreational MDMA dose was an instant quieting of the world. For someone who has lived years with sensory overload issues, I found myself able to walk through a crowded room, tuning out the background noise and not feel overwhelmed. I could smell an orange without feeling dizzy, I could see a crowd as individual people not a chaotic mass of noise, I could eat foods with more than one texture, I could wear clothing with tags in the neck. I could mentally sort noises by importance and tune out the things I didn't need to focus on. For the first time ever, I was able to experience what a quiet world is actually like. I was able to sit down and just enjoy the sound of a world at rest. This wasn't a dulling of all my sensory inputs; it was an increased ability to tune out the static and focus on the important, and that was something I had never experienced before. It was turning down the static dial, but keeping the important information up full. While these aspects of respite from autism were strongest during the high from the drug, they persisted after the high had ended, allowing me to enjoy a few days of a world finally quiet. They gave me the quiet space to reflect on my mind, and to appreciate how much I have to push through in life. I was initially distressed by the realisation that I would have to go back to a world of sensory overload once the drug was out of my system. A friend got me to see that conversely, until then I'd lived my whole life not knowing I could ever get this kind of respite from sensory overload and other autistic spectrum symptoms. Rather than focus on it being sad the world would get loud again, I could be glad I now knew I could theoretically have moments of respite in the future.

Now, this all sounds like the setup to a tale of addiction: an illegal wonder chemical that seems like it can solve all your problems with no drawbacks is a recipe for habitual behaviour and addiction. However, there were a few aspects of the drug itself that allowed me to avoid getting into a cycle of self-destructive addictive behaviour with it. MDMA as a drug works by basically using up all of the brain's stores of chemicals like serotonin at once, meaning that repeated habitual usage drastically diminishes the effectiveness of its results. It's a drug that, if abused by repeated usage, will just stop being effective no matter how much of it you consume. This acted as a remarkably strong failsafe to dissuade making use of it to get through day to day. If you take MDMA let's say three or four days back to back, by the final day you'll find it's creating far less of a high, with a far shorter duration, and a far faster drop off to sobriety. You can physically feel a tolerance building up over just a couple of days, and that in and of itself makes it very easy to see its lack of suitability for use as a day–to-day coping tool. On top of that, the drug causes massively dilated pupils, a sign of drug usage which is incredibly tough to hide. As a result, there were very clear signs that would make my usage obvious, and highlighted the need to be careful about when and how it was consumed. It's not the kind of thing you can subtly consume a little of to 'take the edge off' a social situation, which makes it easier to avoid the alcohol mainstay of 'just one drink before I go out so I'm socially relaxed'. Lastly, unlike stimming, alcohol, caffeine or obsessive organisation, MDMA's effects didn't vanish completely when the chemical had left my system. Changes made by taking the drug once stayed around long term, and provided long-term relief to some of my symptoms. I didn't have to regularly take the drug in order to maintain many aspects of the relief it provided me. Many of the effects of taking MDMA in my 20s stuck around months and months, some even persisting to this day.

First, my willingness to open up about how I feel, as well as starting conversations in general with people, increased dramatically. I expected that during the high itself: a desire to talk to everyone and make everyone my new best friend. I did not expect a long-term increase in ability to communicate with others. I grew up, like many people with autism, somewhat locked in my own head. I went years refusing to open up to my own family in spite of their actively supportive nature, and tried to carry any issues in life on my own shoulders. I knew how overwhelming I found these problems, and I expected them to stress my family in the same way (they're neurotypical, so probably not). I went well into my adulthood not being proactively communicative with those I grew up with, even when I actively needed help. In the long stretch of time since taking MDMA, I've found myself going out of my way to see how my family is doing. I've gone out of my way to start small-talk conversations with them, and not ones pre-planned with a flow chart. I've gone to my parents with things that worry me and asked for their advice, as adults I know I can trust and be open with. I've started really communicating with them in a meaningful way. I've started going out to social events in crowded venues, completely sober, and not being afraid to talk to new people. I now start conversations with people I barely know, and make long-term friends, something I never felt comfortable doing before. I've been able to shut out the mentally addictive pull of obsessively refreshing social media, which has freed up so much of my head in a given day. I can now eat foods with multiple textures, something I was never able to do before. I can eat pineapple, cucumber, allergic yellow peppers, celery, dried mango, grapes and a whole host of other foods that previously made me gag.

Lastly, I realised how thankful I am to be autistic, at least in one area of my life. I realised how terrifyingly quiet the world actually is as a result of taking MDMA, and how much of my willingness to be alone is thanks to living with autism. The world itself is quiet, and that quiet can be terrifying to experience alone. Me? I live in a world where there's always low-level sound, senses blasted, a lot happening. When you live life in static, it's hard to ever feel isolated and alone. I've enjoyed being able to get respite from autism when I have company to share that respite with. I would not want to be neurotypical when alone. It just seems so unbelievably lonely living in a world not filled with that static. It's not a drug I would ever want to consume alone, because a world without the constant static of autism is actually terribly isolating. It's not a world I would feel compelled to live every day of my life in.

However, as much as I may have just spent a lot of words waffling on about how great MDMA is, I can't deny I am addicted to it. I am a drug addict still, to this day, as a result of having taken MDMA. Sure, I'm not the scary kind of drug addict; I'm not taking increasingly large amounts of drugs and putting myself at risk of a fatal overdose, nor am I facing any financial hardships as a result of substance usage, but I am still a drug addict. I may not take MDMA on a daily basis, but I sure as hell think about doing so daily. Every day, at some point in the day, a small part of me thinks about taking MDMA. I can rationally tell myself it's not a good idea, that I shouldn't because I am at work, or it'll be noticeable, or because taking it alone is a telltale sign of addiction, but the thought is there every day of my life, and it takes willpower to ignore. MDMA has made some positive long-term changes to my brain, and has made living with autism undeniably easier in my everyday life, but the sheer strength of its autism-relief properties when actually mid-high is incredibly powerful, and something tough to resist the allure of. Multiple times in my life, I've faced issues of substance addiction, as have many of my friends with autism. While many substances out there, both legal and not, are able to dampen the symptoms of autism, it's easy to crave that period of relief, and that craving of relief can become addiction with relative ease. So many of the coping mechanisms available to autistic individuals are frowned upon by society, or take huge amounts of energy to maintain, and the idea of a quick fix so that you never have to deal with the day–to-day struggle of autism can be incredibly appealing.

In terms of lowering addiction rates in people with autism, we need to tackle the problem from several directions. I feel that stigmatisation of activities like stimming needs to be fought, so that non-chemical coping mechanisms are not something that people are afraid to explore. However, on top of that, we need to support proper research into autism's symptoms, and medication options that can offer relief and respite to those who want it, without having to resort to inebriants. There are clearly chemicals out there that can affect a brain with autism, albeit with side effects, and until we find a treatment that can help calm those symptoms when needed, people are going to regularly turn to illegal or context-inappropriate, potentially addictive ways of self-medicating the days where their symptoms are just a bit too much to bear. Lastly, we need understanding and compassion for individuals with autism who struggle with issues of addiction. If people could look at people with autism who use substances like MDMA or alcohol to manage their symptoms from time to time, understand that they're trying to find respite from a condition that never switches off and has no official treatment options and sympathise with the difficulty of that situation, it would make it easier to have honest conversations about the things that drive that addiction, and how to safely walk the line between occasional respite and life-impacting addiction.

I am lucky, in that I'm a drug addict whose addiction is under control. I think about illegal drugs on a daily basis, but I certainly do not act on that daily urge to consume class A drugs. I don't use drugs alone, I don't use drugs to a financially detrimental extent and I don't use them in amounts that risk death by overdose. Still, I am an addict, and I can't deny that fact. I'm someone living with a brain that's never quiet, living with a condition with no official medication available to treat, and until we have a proper conversation about addiction rates in people with autism spectrum conditions, people like me will continue to live, trying to balance their addictions with the urge to find relief from an overwhelming lifelong medical condition.

II

Living through Transition and Diagnosis

CHAPTER 6

Transition, and Learning to Read Who I Wanted to Be

By the time I was in my early 20s, my life as Laura was starting to take proper shape. I was working full time under a female name, with female gender markers on my ID, and presenting as female in every area of my life. I was on hormones, I was speaking to a therapist, I was out to the world and I was starting to live a new life where I could be more direct and open about how I wanted to be perceived. The problem was, I kind of sucked at getting the world to read me as a woman. By the time I started medical transition, taking both hormone blockers to halt testosterone puberty worsening, and taking oestrogen to start feminising some aspects of myself, the bulk of first puberty's damage had already been done. I had dark coarse facial hair growth on my face and neck, I had a ludicrously large Adam's apple, my shoe size was too large for shopping in most women's sections without cramming them into shoes several sizes too small for me and most of my bones were pretty much set for good: I had relatively broad shoulders, narrow hips, a slightly square face and was over six feet tall. These are all pretty common aspects of testosterone puberty, and none of these are things that can be altered without surgery once they've had time to happen in the first place. It's an issue any trans woman who transitions after their first puberty has completed has to live with and learn to handle. When it comes to getting your penis inverted and crafted into a vagina, the NHS generally consider that a necessary treatment for trans women. At least when I was going through the NHS, pretty much everything else was considered an optional cosmetic procedure, and as a result not covered by NHS funding. If you wanted facial feminisation surgery to smooth out your face, or a tracheal shave to reduce Adam's apple prominence, you needed to pay for those out of your own pocket, and they don't come cheap. On top of this, things like facial hair growth and voice changes are not affected by hormones, at least for trans women. Getting on hormones doesn't make your facial hair stop growing, nor does it reduce the depth of your voice. Testosterone is a pretty tricky hormone to deal with, as the changes it makes are more or less permanent and not open to later hormone alteration. Trans men can start taking testosterone and find that facial hair starts to grow and their body shape changes, but starting oestrogen won't convince your body to un-deepen your voice or thin out that facial fuzz. You might get lucky like me and find hormone replacement therapy makes some of your body hair lighter and less noticeable, but that's about it for undoing the changes made by testosterone puberty.

The bigger problem comes into play when you're a trans woman who also suffers with autism, because a lot of the techniques other trans women use in order to present more femininely come with their own set of challenges that can make them inaccessible to women like myself.

My eternal battle with makeup

Let's start with makeup, because it's the bane of my personal existence. I undeniably look more feminine, and experience less anxiety and dysphoria over my appearance, when I wear well-applied makeup. I can use a good foundation to cover up my stubble and mask its appearance, I can use mascara and eyeliner to draw attention to my eyes and I can use lipstick to make my lips appear fuller. Contouring can help disguise the shape of my face, and I have a far lower rate of being misgendered when wearing well-applied makeup. There are however, two major problems when it comes to me wearing makeup: the texture on my skin and the difficulty applying it to my own face.

Let's start with the texture issue. I frequently have to deal with touch-based oversensitivity, and unless I am having a rare day of relief from those symptoms, I tend to find that actually wearing makeup takes up a lot of my mental resources. All I want to do the whole time I am wearing makeup is wipe it off, wash it off, retouch it, perfect it, get it off, touch it to assure myself things are okay, not touch it to not get fixated on it and generally think far too much about the abnormal feeling that's clinging to my face skin.

Then there's actually applying makeup. Like many people on the autism spectrum, I suffer from a multitude of coordination issues. Apparently it's because a key part of coordinating oneself relies on processing visual information accurately in order to process and predict where your body is, then accurately make small movements adjusting to that information. If you've got a brain that's oversensitive to visual information – and as such consistently trying to process too much information – unsure of which bits to focus on and which to filter out, it's going to affect your ability to accurately adjust to that information. In short, too much information in via the eyes means understanding how to make specific movements is harder. I struggle with both small-scale and large-scale motor control, meaning I am frequently clumsy as well as struggle to do detailed tasks like tying my shoes, holding small objects and applying makeup to my face. I don't have the coordination to apply different levels of pressure when applying foundation, meaning I struggle to blend and soften the edges and end up with horribly visible lines around the edges of my face. I can't apply eyeliner evenly, or without poking myself repeatedly in the eyes. I spent years when I first transitioned practising my makeup on a daily basis, but no matter how hard I tried, I just couldn't make my hands do the subtle small movements I needed them to do.

Comfortable clothing is hard to find

As someone who has a lot of issues with touch-based over-sensitivity, finding clothing that works for my body can at times be a challenge. As an autistic adult, I find I have a lot of difficulty with tight, form-fitting clothing, or outfits that feature multiple different types of fabrics. I find that I am oversensitive to a lot of aspects of fabrics and how they fit with my body. It's a big enough area of conflict in my life today; it inspired the name of this book. I struggle with clothing tags, which are made of different material to the clothing they are fitted into, and stick out at odd angles, flapping around unpredictably and poking into me, dragging uncomfortably and taking up all my attention trying to manage. Tight-fitting sections of clothing feel like they're cutting into my skin, and cause a conflict where some of my skin has predictable constants but some areas do not. Thick necklines feel heavy on my skin. Certain materials feel like their fibres are scratching me like a thousand tiny thorns. Some clothing is too flowy and wafty, unpredictable in where it will sit. Some shoulder straps are too prone to falling or shifting. Some clothing rests on the wrong areas, and sets off my organisational tidying obsessions.

Simply put, clothing as a person with an autism spectrum condition can be really tough to manage. While the fact that clothing tags, textures and fit styles can cause problems for individuals on the autism spectrum likely doesn't come as a huge surprise to many of you reading this book, what is rarely talked about is how that texture sensitivity issue with clothing intersects with learning to manage a new clothing wardrobe after coming out as a trans woman. So, here's the deal: when you come out as transgender, one very common issue that comes up is having to very quickly and self-sufficiently develop a new clothing wardrobe from scratch. I had probably spent maybe 16 or more years building a wardrobe, and having one built for me, that emphasised traditionally masculine traits and presented me to the world as male. Every item of clothing I had was sort of selected towards that aim, and it's not until you decide you want to throw that wardrobe out and start over that you realise how herculean a task that is.

First, most people don't develop a full wardrobe at once; they do so item by item over the years. Getting together multiple outfits so you don't appear to only own one set of clothing, enough to cover all occasions that come up and enough items that you can for example fit a dress code if needed is expensive as a proposition for anyone, but it comes with a bunch of additionally complicating factors when you're trans. I didn't know what clothing size I was, I didn't know what style suited me, I didn't know what cuts and fits were flattering, or which clothing items I was buying would pair with others I had at home. I didn't know the terms to describe items I was looking for, and I didn't know if there were stores that would accommodate my unique proportions.

I was also in early transition utterly terrified of the thought of going into a shop and trying on female-coded clothing. A lot of this was because of imagined issues: if I went into a shop and bought something without trying it on, I worried someone serving me would somehow know I was trans, rather than simply assuming I was shopping for a partner. Part of that fear however was based in real negative experiences I had when first trying to shop for clothes. Very early on in transition, I remember visiting a UK outlet store chain that has brand name clothing that is no longer sold in the stores that originally produced them, as well as cheap off-brand items. I went up to the changing area, dressed in a skirt and top, and asked to try on a series of very clearly feminine-coded items. The store staff told me to head into the men's, which I responded to saying I was female. They told me that the men's changing room was the one I would be required to use, so I reluctantly and defeatedly did. The doors in the men's changing areas basically only covered neck to knees, so I had to get changed into a dress while a man standing opposite could very clearly see I was changing into female-coded clothing in the men's room. I quickly changed my mind, put my clothes back on and ran out.

This early encounter put me off actually trying clothes on before buying them for a long time, which is a big part of why I bought so many of the wrong clothes early in my transition. I ended up buying a lot of clothing that was ill fitting, the wrong size or simply looked ridiculous on me, an exercise in time and money that I could scarcely afford at the time. Part of the issue is that as a trans adult, you are somewhat learning what works for you in a vacuum, without parental support or the support of your peers to help guide you through the process. For most young girls, their parents are able to pass on knowledge and expertise on what looks good on them. Most early outfits are selected by parents, which allows the child to get a sense for matching outfits picked for them. Then, when it's time to start experimenting with clothing themselves, picking their own outfits, they're generally young enough that they can do that experimentation without fear of judgement. They can pick a pretty dress that really doesn't go with that hat they want to wear and it's not a problem that they gave the combination a go.

As a transgender adult, I had to go through that period of experimentation by myself, largely unaided, and I wore some truly trashy outfits that would have looked more at home on an adult more than twice my age, or considerably younger than myself. I wore outfits that were not flattering in the slightest, and I had to do so publicly to learn what worked.

I also lacked the ability to really go through that period of experimentation with my peers. Most of the women I was friends with during my transition had sort of found their clothing style a decade or so before, and many of them were afraid to be too critical of mine for fear of being seen as not encouraging me in my attempts. This led to me not getting proper feedback on my outfit choices, which slowed the process of finding suitable clothes considerably. Basically, when your supportive female friends won't tell you that your outfits look anything other than cute, you don't really learn what works for you.

However, the biggest issue as a transgender woman on the autism spectrum when finding clothes was walking the line between being feminine coded in presentation, and finding clothes that didn't set off my sensory issues. As a trans woman who transitioned post-puberty, I often have an uphill climb to be read as female by people around me, and I find the more I wear clothing that accentuates my body shape the more often I am read as female. The maths is simple: if I wear more items that are traditionally coded as feminine, fewer people refer to me as he, him or sir, and I avoid the dysphoria that comes along with that misgendering. Pair that with the fact that I think I just generally look really nice dressed that way and the choice seems obvious. The problem is, a lot of the clothing I like wearing for those reasons plays havoc with that bit of my brain that stresses over tactile sensory inputs. The first time I wore a bra – stuffed with basically two silicon chicken fillet-style mastectomy breast forms in order to make a dress I wanted to wear sit on me correctly – I had to deal with a whole host of new sensations I had never experienced before. There's the bra straps and clasp, which press tight against the skin and can at times feel like they're physically cutting in to me, even when they're loose and properly fitted enough not to leave huge indentations in my skin. The breast forms added weight on my chest that shifted in ways I could not control, and in the summer heat I sweated enough to cause me a great deal of discomfort. I started wearing scarves to hide my Adam's apple, but the way they gradually shifted and rotated throughout the day made them a constant mental drain, something I had to keep checking on and fixing throughout the day. Tights riding down and not sitting correctly was a distraction that was impossible to ignore, as were strappy tops where the straps shifted around. Clothing suddenly was made of new fabrics and had differing necklines and different cuts. I had a hundred new types of sensory input to process, and it was a lot for me to take in all at once.

For the longest time, my solution to this issue was to basically flip flop my appearance, depending on how difficult I felt the situation I was likely to be in was, and how many people were likely to see me and make assumptions about my gender. If I was working from home or going to the shops, I would wear comfy clothing that I knew inside out, sometimes wearing the same tracksuit trousers, shirt and baggy hoodie for days at a time. I'd focus near exclusively on wearing clothing that worked with my sensory symptoms, assume that I would be misgendered as a result and brace myself accordingly. Then, if someone was going to see me who I wanted to specifically gender me correctly, I'd wear feminine-coded clothing, putting my comfort completely aside in exchange for the better shot at correct gender reading. While this flip flopping took up several years of my life, I eventually found a few compromises which have made finding a middle ground between those two far easier.

Though practised trial and error, I eventually learned some materials and styles of shirts and trousers that manage to feminine code me, while still working with my sensory issues. I can now wear female cut t-shirts and hareem trousers together, remaining comfortable without removing my feminine coding. One of the best discoveries I made that helped me combat this problem was the prevalence in recent years of cheaply available female-coded stimming jewellery. Now most days when I go out I acessorise my outfit with a stimming ring, which helps feminine code me while allowing me something to sit and fiddle with if I am getting overwhelmed by the rest of my outfit. I wear a bracelet that I can chew on, and another bracelet that I can twist and twirl and rotate, both of which are coded in pinks, purples and blues that seem to help me being read as female, even when the rest of my outfit is a bit baggy and shapeless.

By combining feminine coding with autism-stimming utility, these accessories have been a life saver for me on days when I want to avoid misgendering, but also only feel up to wearing a baggy shirt and leggings.

As a counterpart to the discovery of stim jewellery accessories was the discovery of clothing specifically targeted at autism, which in many places allowed me to engage with items I normally could not find versions of that worked for me. From seamless socks, which avoid irritating shifting in my shoes, to women's fit t-shirts made without tags or seams present from the start, realising there were options I could add to my wardrobe rotation for days I found tough was deeply rewarding. Bralettes don't feature fastenings, can be found without tags and create an area of consistent and gentle pressure without pushing uncomfortably on certain lines of my chest. Their material is consistent and predictable, and it's a solution that's fast becoming a much needed lifeline in my sensory world. Until the day the world designs autism-friendly bras with reduced seams, wider bands, correctly textured fabrics and even pressure, this is probably the closest I'm going to find to a workable option. Post-lower surgery, without a pesky penis complicating things, I can now make use of seamless compression underwear, which sit reliably in position, don't have seams moving around all the time and provide calming, predictable sensory information in much the same way weighted blankets do. Leggings post-lower surgery give me a clothing option that stays in place, doesn't move around, is often made out of materials that don't conflict with my sensory issues and highlights that my crotch is flat, helping to further improve my odds of being read as female at a glance.

Finding smells that calm my senses, like the scent of cinnamon or lavender, was also incredibly helpful for getting used to uncomfortable clothing. I found scented sprays in both fragrances and, for a few years, would heavily douse new clothing in those smells, then let them air out a little before wearing them for the first time. While people must have thought me a little odd showing up smelling strongly of spices or like a floral air freshener, it helped me to have a positive calming sensory experience tied to an item of clothing while I got used to the unique tactile experiences of that item.

These are the kinds of discoveries that ultimately helped me begin to manage walking the line between autism-friendly clothing and female-coded clothing, finding items specifically designed to suit autistic women and finding stimming items that are female-coded, paired with simple practice and repetition with clothing styles I found uncomfortable previously. It took me several years, but I am already far more at ease balancing these than I was maybe four years ago. I just wish I'd had some tailored advice on how to get here a little bit sooner than I did.

There's this sort of fear instilled in trans women from when our transition begins that, if we don't dive head first into femininity of appearance, we will suffer as a result. This belief is instilled in many of us early on in transition, when starting to seek early medical support. I remember hearing horror stories of trans women going to the gender identity clinic in jeans and a hoodie, an outfit combo many cis women regularly wear, and being told that because of the way they were dressed, the doctor did not believe they were sincere in feeling dysphoric. As shocking as those kinds of stories are initially to hear, they did line up with my own lived experiences. If I was going somewhere and wanted to be taken seriously as a woman, I had to show up in a blouse, skirt and cardigan. Where mainstream feminism has spent the past few decades fighting for the right of cis women to wear anything they like and not be seen as less female for it, with regards to trans women, if we're not wearing a dress we're not trying hard enough to be female, or we don't want it enough, and it's seen as carte blanche for harassment and hassle. Equally, if we do wear dresses and skirts, we're accused of performative femininity, of believing female identity is nothing more than the dress or skirt being worn. It's a bit of a nasty double-edged sword trans women have to live with. Learning to walk that line took me several years. I quite like butch lesbian aesthetics, but learning how close to that line I could walk without just being read as male was a considerable task. It made me afraid to wear clothing that worked comfortably with my touch sensitivity for the longest time.

Learning to read subtly coded mannerisms

As a woman living with autism, I really struggle with reading small nonverbal aspects of communication. It's not that I can't see a smile or a frown; it's just that noticing a small upturn at the sides of a mouth, in the static of all the other sensory information bombarding me day to day, takes a lot of energy and focus. What this meant for me was that all those little differences in the ways men and women tend to hold themselves, walk and sit, the differences in vocal intonation, the differences in vocal pacing, were very hard for me to pick up on and learn to emulate. Most people learn these little micro gestures naturally over the course of their lives, and trying to force yourself to learn them is tough for anyone, but with an autism spectrum condition it can be an even greater challenge. What this all meant when added together was that, while I was feeling better about my gender identity as a result of transitioning, I found presenting myself femininely took a great deal of mental effort, often caused me distress with my autism symptoms and initially revolved around a great deal of deliberate actions taken in an attempt to blend in.

With regard to my voice, I never got formal voice training. The way I learned to change my voice, as well as improve the feminine qualities of my voice, was by recording and editing my own podcasts. I would record myself talking with friends for an hour, then spend the next day editing the audio, listening intently to my speech, while reading an online list of feminine vocal traits. I would listen to sentences I had said over and over, in isolation, asking myself if I was raising my tone in the right places, if my voice sounded natural or strained, if I was raising and lowering my pitch as I spoke or staying monotone. I would listen to my voice, read a checklist and try to assess in an analytical isolated context whether my voice sounded feminine enough. I did this three times a week, every week, until over time I just sort of picked things up. While changing my vocal mannerisms was initially a huge amount of consistent effort, years later it has become my new normal. I now have to make a concerted effort to make my voice anything like it used to be.

In terms of the non-speaking mannerisms, I found these a lot harder to learn. I ended up spending a lot of time watching videos on YouTube of people animating female character models for video games. The looping nature of the animations meant I could just try and soak in a mannerism as much as possible, and it avoided the issue of people watching out in the wild and having someone get aggressive at me for staring at them.

But, in the end, over the course of a few years, I found a method that worked even better for me. I tried just not giving a shit. In early transition I actively pushed for femme presentation all the time with all the mental drain that came with it. This was partly to combat my feelings of dysphoria, and partly because I had heard horror stories of the NHS refusing to treat trans patients if they didn't present as an exaggerated caricature of their target gender. Over time, I started to think 'You know what, women are allowed to wear tracksuit bottoms and baggy hoodies; they might not emphasise my femininity, but some days I'll take that hit for autism comfort.' Similarly, there are days my skin feels too sensitive to shave, and I honestly just don't. Body and facial hair happen in cis women too, and if nobody important is going to see my face that day, it's okay not to worry about it.

This no longer caring attitude is what carried me through later months and years, when my sensory issues flared up.

I knew I could get away with leaving some traditionally feminine aspects of myself to one side, if I needed to just be comfy and not anxious about the sensory inputs on my body. That road, however, took a long time, because my autism specific needs, and my needs as a trans woman, were so clearly in direct conflict with each other.

Learning to be one of the gals

Back when I still intended to hide the fact I was trans, in early transition, it always became awkward any time conversations of my childhood arose, as I had to on the fly tweak and rewrite history to better fit the version I wanted the world to see. I remember once in early transition, working in a retail store, having a customer sort of half recognise me, and ask me if I had a brother who used to work at the store. While it was clear they'd mistaken pre- and post-transition me as two separate people, I spun them some nonsense story about how my brother had moved to London and wouldn't be working there any more. These were the sorts of lies I told here and there to make sense of my dropping into life as a woman out of nowhere as a young adult. I found myself forcing myself to laugh along at things I didn't understand; I had to dodge my way around direct questions, and it was all just a bit of a rough time.

Thankfully, I found a really great group of female friends through costume design in my late teens and early 20s, and they were not only aware I was trans, but willing to bend over backwards to accommodate helping me feel at home. They didn't treat my lack of going through periods as a teen as something that made me less of a woman. They didn't judge me for not knowing sleepover etiquette; they just let me ask questions without ever questioning my identity, which was exactly what I needed at that time. All too often in the media, we see trans women portrayed as 'men pretending to be women', but ultimately the opposite is far more accurate. As a trans woman, I wasn't pretending to be female when I started presenting myself as female; I was learning to drop a carefully rehearsed act, and that was part of what was so tough.

In previous chapters in this book, I've talked about how learning to survive autism symptoms was performative. I made flowcharts, I assessed actions and likely outcomes, I presented a version of myself that could get through the world unharmed; well, that's what I was also doing with regards to gendered presentation prior to transition. I learned that holding myself in a certain way, making my voice sound a certain way, not acting in certain ways, could prevent me getting harassed. I spent years methodically pretending to be a man, only to come out and, with the right group of friends, just let myself start to unwind and be more authentically myself. I had to learn a lot of performative femininity to avoid harassment and NHS gatekeeping, but ultimately I just relaxed and let myself be who I was. I ended up finding that the best way to find who I wanted to be.

As it turns out, the best way to learn to be who I was was to just drop the facade, and let myself be myself. The best friends I've ever had are the ones I can just be me with, whoever that is, and still be seen as the woman I am.

CHAPTER 7

Squeezing a Late Youth into Adulthood

One near universal experience common to pretty much any adult who transitions once out in the world, rather than transitioning during their school years, is experiencing a second attempt at childhood. Usually manifesting as a sort of spiritual return to one's teenage years, you'll often see trans people spend a few years once they're comfortable and established in their new life role being experimental and silly, taking risks and connecting with activities generally considered age inappropriate for them. It's kind of an understandable thing, and something I know I have undeniably done a lot of over the past few years, and my whole life really. It's totally healthy when done right, and fulfills a few needs that are present for people who've transitioned in their adulthood.

First, there's a medical reason a lot of us go through a bit of a teenage spell as adults: second puberty. I've not really talked a lot in this book about the medical changes I've chosen to undergo as part of my transition, because ultimately I don't really think they're important to anyone but myself.

Getting surgery to change my penis into a vagina gave me the comfort to wear swimwear and leggings. Hormones changed my emotional range a bit, and are slowly changing my body shape. That's the basics of the changes I personally made, but not every trans woman makes those same changes, and their reasons are their own. However, as someone who did undergo hormone replacement therapy (HRT), where I took one set of medications to block testosterone's effect on my body and began taking oestrogen tablets, I did experience a second puberty.

If you've been through puberty once already, you probably remember what it was like. A maelstrom of confusion, pain, exhaustion, urges and change. You've got body parts where you didn't before, you've got interests you didn't have before and you're constantly running on full emotional blast. Second puberty for me, as for a lot of trans people, was much the same. I found myself being attracted to people I was not attracted to before, I found myself crying all of the time at everything and I found myself experiencing growing pains as parts of me began to change. Much like cis women, my hormone levels fluctuate in cycles across the month, so I'll have some overly emotional days towards the end of the month, and I have to be aware of that in ways I didn't have to with testosterone. The big difference for me as a trans woman between these two puberties was that the first one I experienced was nothing but negative; it was years of my body changing and me being upset and terrified at that notion. The second, on the other hand, was positive. Sure, it was tiring and emotionally overwhelming, but it was positive. I had all these changes happening, and the urge to seize all the opportunities I never felt able to in my first teen years. I wanted to show off my skin. I wanted to spend time outside with friends. I wanted to experiment and try new things. I wanted to introduce myself to new people. I wanted to take the time to discover who I was. My second puberty was a time of huge self-discovery, and a lot of the things people want to do in order to explore who they are happen to be things generally associated with people in their late teen years. We just kind of get to them a bit late.

Putting aside the medicinal aspect, probably the far bigger factor in trans adults embracing traditionally more youthful aspects of life is the feeling that there's a lot of things we ultimately missed out on our chance to do. I was living as male during pretty much my entire childhood, and there were a lot of aspects of childhood I kind of just had to watch from the outside: gossipy sleepovers, going out clothes shopping, simply walking platonically holding hands with a friend, singing songs as you skip down the street. These are all really simple things, but when they're seemingly kept away from you for arbitrary reasons, there's a real urge to engage with them when you're finally able. I have a couple of friends, Becky and Makeda, who have been incredibly helpful in my life at allowing me to basically get around to these things a little late, without judgement. We've had adult, giggly gossip sleepovers. We've skipped down the street arm in arm laughing. We've gone shopping together as a group. I've thankfully had a chance, as an adult, to engage with some of the activities I missed out on my chance to do.

Much earlier in this book, I mentioned asking my parents

for a paper doll, like the one they had made for my sister, a request they twisted to something more socially acceptable. As an adult, I will occasionally just buy myself a cute female-coded toy or doll. Not because I need it, but because I can. I'm at a place in my life where I am able to, guilt free, engage with things I was unable to as a child who had been assigned male.

I was stopped from dancing out of fear that I would be bullied by my male peers. Now I go out dancing a couple of times a month. I'm reclaiming feminine-coded activities that my childhood denied me, because being an adult doesn't mean I can't embrace and support the little girl inside me who just wanted to dance and play with dolls like her sister. I own stuffed animals as an adult, and proudly give them pride of place in the bedroom my partner and I share, because I'm at a place in my life where my friends won't judge me for sometimes wanting to just hug something cute and cuddly. I'm living out aspects of feminine-coded childhood as an adult, because a few decades ago there was a little girl living in this body who wasn't allowed to explore those aspects of life.

On top of that, there's also the part that romance plays in reliving your wild and crazy teen years, but as an adult with same-sex attractions. I didn't view myself as holding same-sex attractions until I was a little way into transitioning to female. I knew that my whole life I had been primarily attracted to women, but my dating life had been held back by my own lack of awareness over who I wanted to be. Before coming out as trans, I felt awkward and uncomfortable dating, because while I was dating the people I wanted to, I was not doing so the way

I wanted. The *who* I was dating was right, but the who I was dating *as* was wrong. When I came out as trans and reframed my relationships with women as being same-sex relationships, it changed so much about the mechanics of dating, and my place in that world, that I felt like I was dating for the first time all over again. Also those awkward shy 'is it okay if I tell you I think I might like you' interactions that are usually gone and out the way before someone hits their 20s were a big part of how I engaged with romance. I was still anxious and new, trying to work out who I was, who I liked and what I liked in a relationship, and I was doing it considerably later than my peers.

Outside of that, there's also being on the autism spectrum, and the effect that can have for many individuals. I, like many people on the autism spectrum, sort of felt the need to mature before my time. I was societally shunned by my peers; people my age just wanted nothing to do with me, and my obsessive urge to learn meant I often wanted to engage on topics in ways that did not connect properly with those around me. As a result, I am one of the many people on the autism spectrum who grew up very early in an attempt to find connection and solace in adults instead, people who might be more willing to look past my awkwardness. The problem with that is two-fold. I sort of skipped my chance to be a carefree child; I wasn't allowed to engage with my peers, and even when I was, I was often too anxious to, jumping straight to behaving properly and following the rules religiously. Second, as addressed earlier in this book, trying to engage with adults at times put me in traumatic situations, and those traumatic events when paired with bullying from my peers forced me to grow up and mature early as a coping mechanism. Trauma forces you to grow up fast, because it robs a person of some degree of innocent positive naivety.

When you add all these together, and look at LGBT trans women on the autism spectrum, it's no surprise that so many of us engage with aspects of childhood well into our adulthoods. We're forced to grow up fast by peers who don't understand us, we're denied aspects of childhood we have to look in on from outside and we're often unable to experience teenage puppy love at an appropriate time.

People like me often get into our 20s or older, transition, and find the world suddenly open to us. Suddenly we're positive; we've got a handle on our lives, we know who we are and want to share that with the world, regardless of what they think. Suddenly we have freedom, and money, and friends who understand what we missed out on. I don't think it's a huge surprise that some of us just quietly want to act a little young, silly and carefree once we get to grips with who we are. We just want some space to make silly voices, take some risks, wear something garish and dance around the living room without a care in the world.

CHAPTER 8

I'm Proud I'm not Invisible

As a trans woman with autism, I'm most palatable to the world when it can pretend I don't exist, and this is something that I want not only to push against myself, but really hope we see the world push back against in the years to come. The world is getting more comfortable with a certain class of trans people. In particular, trans women who can 'pass' as cisgender. But what about those of us who can't pass – or don't think we should have to? Here's to women with prominent Adam's apples, five o'clock shadows and deep voices. Here's to women like me.

In the 1990s, trans women were punchlines: awareness by way of mockery. It felt like we only existed so the hero of *Ace Ventura: Pet Detective* had an excuse to comically vomit at the thought that he might have liked a trans woman, and then forcibly strip off her clothes and out her genitals in front of a crowd of vomiting onlookers. At least someone was acknowledging our existence, right? In that era, trans women in media were usually very feminine – but only to set up the punchline. The big reveal. In the 1990s conception of a trans woman's transition, we simply snuck off for one secretive operation. We'd reappear with bandages on our faces, and slowly unwind the bandage to reveal the most unbelievably, effortlessly gorgeous woman anyone had ever seen.

The trend continued through the 2000s. Popular culture still portrayed trans women as flawlessly beautiful but with a horrible secret – a penis! You heard the transphobic slur 'tranny' everywhere. Trans men got no representation at all. As far as I can tell, comedians found the concept of a 'man' giving up his 'manhood' funnier than they did a 'woman' becoming more 'manly.'

Things got a little better in the 2010s. First, we got our first high-profile examples of trans actors playing trans characters. In *Orange Is the New Black* – the first season, at least – Laverne Cox got to play a nuanced trans woman of colour who suffered for being trans, but also got to be part of a story that wasn't just about her transness. Second, Caitlyn Jenner publicly transitioned and appeared in a glamorous *Vanity Fair* spread. Here's the thing, though. A major reason Cox and Jenner enjoyed the friendly media coverage they did came down to their ability to conform to a traditional standard of female beauty. Trans women who can attain a level of traditionally cisgender female attractiveness – which keeps them from being obviously transgender – are safe and acceptable. Even if their appearance is merely an accident of luck, wealth or the timing of their transition. In reality, most trans women don't look like Laverne Cox or Caitlyn Jenner. Most of us look...well, like trans women. We might have a visible Adam's apple. We might have real trouble hiding that five o'clock shadow. We might have broad shoulders or big hands and feet. We might be really tall or have a deep voice. We might have a penis. We're what's sometimes referred to as 'non-passing'. As trans women, we are told that to gain acceptance, we have to pass for cisgender. We have to be invisible. We have to be indistinguishable from someone who was assigned female at birth. We are the trans people who most badly need protection in the world today. We're the people who get the most badly hurt when the government rolls back our rights. We are the trans people you don't see in the media. When the media portray non-passing trans women, it's usually cisgender men who play them. Male actors win awards for their courage in playing trans women. In truth, they're just reflecting back at the world what the world assumes trans women are. We're not women. We're just men in dresses. That's the message that the media today tries to send. The media wrongly depicts us as makeup-obsessed little boys who made a choice one day to become women. We're never just women who happen to possess some untraditionally feminine attributes.

But here's how things are changing for the better. Non-passing trans women enjoy wider acceptance when more high-profile trans women come out publicly – and don't make an effort to 'pass'. The more non-passing trans people in the popular consciousness, the closer we march to the day when the general population of the world take the non-passing trans population as seriously as they do the high-profile passing population. It's already happening. Laura Jane Grace, the lead singer of Against Me!, came out publicly in one recent album, packed her next album with angry trans anthems...and didn't change her voice! That gave deeper-voiced trans women hope that the wider population might one day take them seriously, too.

Honestly, I don't pass very well. My voice falters. My stubble is visible late in the day. I'm over six feet tall and I struggle with traditionally feminine movements and mannerisms. I spent a long time trying incredibly hard to pass. I eventually stopped trying. I started posting selfies in which I had visible facial hair or where I'd tied my hair back, exposing more of my traditionally masculine facial structure. I stopped wearing scarves that disguised my manly neckline.

I'm glad I did. I honestly think the world needs more trans people who are open about their transitions. Who don't try to pass. Who insist that beautiful can mean a lot of different things. The same goes for autism and how it's seen in the world. People with autism are seen as valuable if we can do something truly amazing – we're talking those rare savant-level abilities – or if we can keep our issues hidden well enough to get through the day unnoticed. Basically we either have to have superpowers or be invisible. We're portrayed in media as being visibly symptomatic only when that can be offset with some genius ability that justifies our right to be allowed to be a bit different. We get portrayals of characters like Sheldon Cooper in *The Big Bang Theory* who is permitted to be obsessed with routine and structure and rules and organisation, because he's the smartest person in any given room by a country mile. He's also offset with goofy silly catchphrases, like 'Bazinga', to make his quirks appear charming and fun. We're not allowed to exist as normal. We're not allowed to exist as people who are a little different, but just like anyone else are trying to live an average kind of life, get by day to day and make do. We're not allowed to be normal people who occasionally need to flap our hands back and forth to calm down. We're definitely not allowed to exist as LGBT and on the autism spectrum at the same time; that's way too many forbidden things going on. It's too out there: representation gone mad. No person is that many diversity tick boxes at once, are they?

I'm an adult who can't hide my autism and LGBT status. Anyone who knows me long enough will work out that I am trans, I have autism and I experience same-sex attractions. You know what? I'm proud of that. The world may want me to be invisible, but I am proud to be visible, to be known, to be seen.

III

———

Life Post-Transition
and Diagnosis

CHAPTER 9

LGBT Spaces Are not for Autistic Adults

As a member of the LGBT community living with autism, one of the biggest issues I have been unable to find a suitable solution for is meeting and socialising safely with other LGBT people in my local area. You see, being an LGBT adult today still comes with some risks, even living somewhere like England. Men, afraid of being perceived as gay, often lash out at transgender individuals. We're at times perceived as men, or as predatory dangers to society. There are people who recognise my position in society as being a vulnerable one and will try to take advantage of that fact. There are those who stalk me on the street making creepy propositions, those who kick at bathroom doors feeling I should not be using those spaces, and people who mislead me in order to later mock me, all based on my visible LGBT status.

The first time this really sunk in for me was about three months after going full time living as Laura. I was on a coach home from a work event in London, a three-hour bus journey on motorways where stopping the vehicle is tough, and getting off before the journey is done would have left me stranded without an exit strategy. Within around ten minutes of the coach leaving the station, a pair of men approached me as I sat alone at the back of the bus, and attempted to force a snuff vial under my nose. I tried to inform the driver, who took very little interest, simply telling me to tell him if things escalated. Once we'd made it onto the motorway, things did escalate. One of the men came and stood over me, questioning me about my genitals and describing how he imagined my body in graphic detail. He repeatedly stated that I should feel lucky; he thought I was sexy, and according to him nobody else ever would. He asked if he could fuck me in the bus bathroom. I said no. He offered to pay me. I said no. He tried to push me into the bathroom by force, an act not one passenger attempted to stop. I had to push past him, sprint to the front of the bus, and force the driver to pull over and call the police.

I spent 20 minutes sitting in the doorway of the bus before we stopped and the police arrived, eventually locating the men and confirming that the substance they had tried to pressure upon me was an illegal drug which would have impaired my perception. I spent the remaining two hours of my bus ride home just thinking over and over in my head. My status as transgender had made these men feel entitled to not only my body, but to tell me I didn't deserve the interest of anyone but these predatory creeps.

This event was the first, but by no means the last. I've numerous times been attacked, pressured or preyed upon by people who see my transgender status as a threat, or a weakness to take advantage of. For my own safety, I have to be careful who I disclose my same-sex attraction or transgender status to, and finding other people like me in my local area is a vital part of being able to make new friends who I feel safe being around.

Typically, the solution to safely finding other LGBT individuals in an area is to attend specifically LGBT-focused venues and events, in order to ensure that the people you are meeting are people you can safely be yourself around. Go to a gay bar or Pride event, meet some other LGBT people, all done. You can go into those settings confident that who you happen to be won't be an issue, and have the flexibility to get to know people based on their interests and personality instead.

Things are not so easy when you're both LGBT and on the autism spectrum. Most LGBT-focused events and venues are aimed at individuals aged 18 and over, because of our weird societally held beliefs that being gay or transgender is inherently an adult and sexual act, or that being around LGBT people as a child will somehow turn a person gay. A big part of this is due to the history of the LGBT rights movement during decades of open and aggressive persecution. If you look back to the 1950s, gay bars were a safe haven for a community that was not socially accepted, and attacks on LGBT individuals focused on the 'unnatural' nature of their sex lives. LGBT people were not seen as people in love, people being themselves or people harming nobody around them; these bars were raided by police because LGBT people were seen as perverts, deviants and dangerous individuals. As a result, these venues had to stay age segregated in order to avoid accusations that they were targeting young people, which played a considerable role in the growth of LGBT spaces once being gay or trans started to become more socially acceptable. Bars and clubs had time to be established as safe havens, places to hide from a world that was hell bent on persecution, and that status as a safe place to hide from a discriminatory world solidified their position as the defacto place for LGBT people to meet for decades to come.

As an unintended side effect of this, most LGBT venues are focused on activities that are adult in nature. You've got gay bars, clubs and dating events aimed at finding sex and romance, and not a whole lot else on a national scale. Because inviting LGBT youth into private spaces risked giving homophobes ammunition to allege wrongdoing, there was never really any incentive for youth-oriented LGBT spaces to blossom, a problem that has persisted ever since.

Today, we still see a lack of LGBT characters in media targeted at children, because it's still seen that allowing children to casually interact with or perceive LGBT individuals will create that status in youth. Parents, by and large, are unwilling to encourage their children who might be LGBT to meet other LGBT children. This is a problem, because as an individual with autism, I struggle with the sensory aspects of many of those adult-oriented environments: loud music, flashing lights, crowds of people I do not know, a huge number of unknown variables mixed up to create a chaotic sea of sensory overload. Those kinds of venues tend to be my worst nightmare. This issue even permeates all-ages LGBT events, like Pride parades. LGBT events tend to be loud, bright and more than a little chaotic.

I get why LGBT events are this way; so often in life as LBGT individuals we're expected to tone ourselves back, for our own safety and so as not to be viewed poorly by those around us. We live life carefully watching what we say, who we say it to and how we say it. These events and venues are an opportunity to be as loud and proud as we like, revelling in the pure joy of being as visible and unrestrained as we like. This doesn't change the fact that the cornerstone LGBT-centric experiences for meeting new people play havoc with my sensory issues.

On top of that, there's also no guarantee that these heavily advertised events will be safe for me as a trans woman with autism. Because they're so high profile, with all eyes on them, they often attract the wrong kinds of people and create difficult types of situations for me to handle. For example, at London Pride 2018, a group of anti-trans protestors hijacked the Pride parade, eventually managing to secure the lead spot in the parade and spewing hate speech, shouting threats of violence at people like me wearing trans Pride flags and calling trans women rapists. In that particular example, I was trapped in a large, busy, sensory-overloaded crowd of people, as a woman from a clearly anti-trans group came up to shout at me that I was a monster. I was scared and overwhelmed, and in my attempt to manage the situation, I told her to fuck off, told her that hate speech wasn't welcome there. She grabbed a police officer and tried to have me arrested. It was an awful lot to try to contend with at that time, with both my status as a trans person and an adult with autism contributing to the stress I faced. This sort of protest appearance is more common when an event for LGBT people is large in scale, and publicly built up long in advance.

Looking a little more broadly at the issue of venues and events being autism aware, autism-friendly events tend to be very one size fits all and inflexible. The best example I have of this is autism-friendly cinema screenings. As an adult living with an autism spectrum condition which largely affects my sensory processing abilities, there are certain aspects of visiting a cinema that always hinder my experience no matter what I do. Bright green neon emergency exit signs always exist in my peripheral vision, I cannot guarantee a seat that isn't directly next to another paying customer, I cannot rewind the film if I missed something important due to there being too much sensory information and I can't control the volume of the film if I am struggling to focus on sounds properly. These are known parts of the cinema-going experience, and I do what I can on a personal level to mitigate those issues. What I don't however do as a method of improving my experience is attend specially marked autism-friendly screenings of movies. I routinely get them recommended to me by friends and family members without autism who've seen them mentioned in passing but not looked properly into what they are. The concept is often misunderstood at a core level. This is not because autism-friendly screenings are inherently bad things; quite the contrary. I don't attend autism-friendly screenings because autism is a spectrum, and the one size fits all approach of autism screenings is tailored to one type of individual with autism over another. Again, this isn't to say the current form in which they exist is flawed. They currently exist in a form beneficial to many, but by no means all, and I want to take the time to explain why their marketing is a little misleading conceptually.

Taking UK cinema chains Odeon and Vue as example cases, both cinemas do offer some potentially beneficial changes as part of their autism-friendly screenings. In isolation, the idea of slight room lighting does help me, in that it makes the exit door lights less comparatively bright and more easily ignorable while watching the film. The ability to openly bring in my own texture-friendly food and drink is useful, but if I'm being honest I do that anyway in regular screenings. A lack of adverts, while not a huge change, does allow me to more accurately predict when a film will end, and makes me more comfortable slotting it into my day, and slightly reduced audio volume levels do make it a little easier for me to focus on the film.

However, a lot of additional factors are introduced by the nature of an autism-friendly screening that are definitely not to my benefit, most notably, the presence of other individuals with autism. While lower volume and higher ambient light are useful in isolation, when paired with the additional movement and noises that accompany an autism-targeted audience I end up being more aware of the sensory information created by my fellow attendees. People moving and making noises is extra information, not drowned out by the lack of light or the high volume, and can ultimately make it harder for me to focus. As much as I struggle with loud single source volume, I struggle more with multiple sources of sensory information

I cannot predict. Also of note, autism-friendly screenings are almost exclusively for films with U and PG ratings, which limits the range of films available that someone like me can experience in that environment. Cutting to the chase, autism-friendly screenings are really screenings designed primarily for young or nonverbal individuals with autism and their families. That's by no means a problem. The lighting and volume changes in those screenings are definitely beneficial, and a heightened tolerance for volume and movement likely mean those accompanying the individual with autism do not need to be as self-conscious while watching the film. They're just not one size fits all experiences.

If I as an adult could attend an autism-friendly screening with the same lighting and volume changes, the same alterations to food and drink policy, but a wider variety of movie types available and the knowledge that I was attending with other adults who were, like me, wanting to avoid sensory distraction, I would probably attend those fairly regularly. As it currently stands, I just sneak my own food in, try to place my hand so it blocks out the exit light, pop in earplugs to dampen noise and hope the seat next to me stays empty. Autism-friendly screenings exist, and I am glad they do, but if your friend with autism would rather not attend one, it may be because much like the autism spectrum itself, these screenings are not one size fits all. The cinema variables are all correct and beneficial in isolation, but do not help me when practically applied.

This is part of the issue when trying to suggest ideas for making LGBT spaces more autism friendly; what is useful for one individual on the spectrum may not help another, and finding ways to improve that experience for a wider number of people can be tricky. One major solution to the lack of autism-friendly LGBT spaces, rather than trying to reform and make room within existing spaces, is to push for a wider variety of LGBT spaces, ones in settings that tend to be less intense on the senses. While I know LGBT cafes exist, as dedicated social groups, they're certainly not as common as gay bars are, which is a real shame. A cafe environment for example offers quieter spaces, a less busy environment, more flexibility about how to engage with the venue and is more accessible to a wider variety of people.

For me and many other LGBT individuals with autism, the internet has been a socialising goldmine, filling in the gap left by our inability to engage with other LGBT spaces. Online, tone of voice and nonverbal facial expressions are removed as factors from understanding conversational intent, with words alone explaining intent. Social media allows me to socialise with other LGBT people, regardless of their location, while controlling my sensory information. I can listen to my own music on loop, eat my texture-limited foods, in comfortable clothing, under a weighted blanket, in my own home while making a new friend who communicates by saying the words they mean directly. Communication online does avoid many of the barriers presented by LGBT bars and Pride events, but it does crucially lack an in-person connection element. Over the years, many have assumed due to my frequent isolation that I do not need in-person company to be happy and comfortable.

Far from it, while I need to initiate it on my terms, I do still need social energy in my life, and it's a shame that online communication with other LGBT people doesn't always provide that.

There are also Pride events in the UK attempting to make accommodations to support individuals with autism. For example, a group called MyUmbrella attended Reading Pride in 2018, and provided space for individuals who were experiencing sensory overload to get away and calm themselves. They had a tent with air beds for people to come sit down on, away from the crowds and the noise, and take a moment to compose themselves in an environment where stimming would not draw any unwanted attention. On a connected note, due to the overlap with gender dysphoria, the group also offered private changing areas for transgender individuals, so that anyone attending Pride who needed to change before or after their journey for safety would have a place to handle sorting their clothing in peace and comfort. The group is hoping to expand to more Pride events nationally in 2019, and their approach certainly wouldn't be unappreciated at these events.

Additionally, while London doesn't currently have any LGBT community centres, at least at the time of writing, they're soon to be getting their first as a result of a huge online crowdfunding campaign. The fund, which raised over £100,000, would offer an all-ages, alcohol-free space for LGBT people to meet and socialise in safety, as well as away from the barriers posed by venues for over 18s. The idea is that the venue would be open from morning until night, be free to enter and be free of loud noise and alcohol use. The money is being used to prove demand for the space, to help bring in larger donors from elsewhere. The hope is that over time more cities will follow suit, offering these kinds of spaces, making them something that is considered a normal part of life rather than a rare oddity.

Considering the statistically high overlap between autism and LGBT status, it would be nice to see a proper conversation begin about how to support LGBT individuals with autism in their attempts to socialise, but until then small charity setups and the internet are the only real options that work for me personally.

CHAPTER 10

Transgender Conflicts and Autism

As a trans woman living in the UK, I often find myself having to handle difficult social situations, requiring nuance in how they are responded to. If I enter a single gender women's bathroom, and someone stops me to tell me the men's bathroom is in the other direction, I have to make a judgement on the person who has stopped me. Are they stopping me because they have clocked that I am a trans woman, they do not believe trans women are valid as women and they want me to leave because of that? If so, do I fight my ground? Do I provide ID like my passport, which thankfully lists me as female? Will doing so be sufficient proof to them or just leave me further entrenched in an argument? Should I even feel the need to? If they get aggressive and threaten violence in my presence should I shut myself into a cubicle away from them? Should I run? Would obeying that thought in the back of my mind telling me to just flash my vagina as an act of defiance get them to back off, or simply further the incorrect belief that having lower surgery is a requirement to being taken seriously as a trans woman? Or, on a completely different tack, would just simply saying I am a woman be enough? Would they apologise, trust that I know myself best, and let me go about my business embarrassed that they had incorrectly misread my gender presentation? Would the staff in the venue defend my right to be there? Would they be trained enough in trans rights to know my rights? Would I be safe until venue staff arrived? Do I have friends nearby? Would the defence of a cis woman coming in and telling them to back off be enough to protect me, or would it just put that friend at risk?

Responses to the existence of transgender people vary wildly from person to person currently, in the UK and across the world, and as a result these situations are difficult to manage at the best of times. There's a delicate balancing act to any interaction, the line of reading if a judgement on my appearance is a mistake made in good faith, or an act of agg-ression designed to force me into an unsafe situation, and being able to tell the difference ultimately decides my safety in a lot of different situations. I have to rely on knowing when I am safe and in a position to correct and teach, when I am in a position where I need to fight for my rights, and when the safest thing to do is to hide, putting my own rights aside for the sake of staying safe in a given moment.

When you're also on the autism spectrum, reading these situations with nuance can become even more difficult. I struggle often to read the more nuanced, unspoken aspects of social interactions accurately. When looking at a person's face, there are thousands of bits of data every second, and my brain struggles to hone in on what is important and tune out what is not. In the chaotic storm of static information being generated all the time, I often don't know what to look out for, and struggle to know the intent behind something said in the moment. If someone does an exaggerated smile or frown, I can look at that expression and tell you it's a smile or a frown and the emotion connected to that, but in a fast-moving conversation outside of a testing environment, with someone I do not already know, I often struggle to contextualise the little shifts in tone of voice, the facial expression and posture clues, to tell if they pose a threat or are safe.

As a result, I've had to live a lot of my life post-transition assuming the worst possible outcome from social situations, and adapt accordingly. If I'm having a day where I've had to wear clothing that is not actively feminine coded, and not been able to wear makeup or shave due to tactile sensitivity issues, I have to assume for my safety that I am going to be read as male, and put into situations where I will have to defend my ability to use those spaces. If I can enter those situations alongside other women, or have the mental energy to use my ID to fight my ground, I may still use female-coded spaces, but if I am alone and having a rough day there are occasionally rare times where I have to face defeat and use male-coded spaces instead. Male-coded spaces still pose risks to me as a trans woman, but sometimes that will seem a lesser risk than entering a female-coded space and risking being confronted by someone who does not have my best interests at heart.

If I am using a women's bathroom alone, I will usually

keep my passport in an easily accessible pocket of my bag, so I know it's there if I need to use it to defend myself. If someone seems like they are going to get aggressive, to be safe I tend to leave the bathroom and try again later. In some ways more difficult to handle are the situations in which I face anger and aggression once already inside a cubicle. If someone starts pounding or kicking at the door, or shouting threatening and derogatory terms at me, I will tend to assume that their threats are real. Perhaps they're just trying to scare me, but I err on the side of protecting my safety. I'll try to wait them out as best I can, but that can be tough to do emotionally. In an ideal world, I would handle those moments by putting on some headphones, getting out stimming tools like a fidget cube, tub of slime or rubix cube, and just repeatedly engage in known sensory tasks until I calmed down and the situation was over. Put a song on repeat, solve a cube over and over and keep the anxiety at bay. The problem is that doing so isn't safe when under threat of attack. If the person gets past the door somehow, I have to know what's happening and be able to start moving very quickly if an opportunity to exit safely presents itself. The sensory information of being threatened through a door might be overwhelming, but I have to manage and endure it without my normal coping tools, just in case the worst happens and I need to run.

This is sort of a theme that permeates a lot of difficult situations encountered as a trans woman with autism; the normal autism coping tools at my disposal are not safe to engage in when you're being attacked for your trans woman status.

If I'm being followed through London late at night by a man who started off offering to pay me for sex, then when I refused his offer starts threatening to take it by force, I can't put a song full volume on loop in my headphones because I need to hear what he says. I can't stop and take time to obsessively plan a route home that gets away from him, or gets me to a 24-hour establishment, or gets me near people and cameras, because I have to look like I already know what I am doing and that I am heading somewhere with purpose. I can't use stimming aids or engage in stimming actions, because that gives away my status as a vulnerable member of society who is not confident in their ability to safely escape the situation. I have to handle a difficult social situation without the tools I need to get through non-stressful situations. The situation is tougher and my tools are reduced. It's a deeply unpleasant experience to encounter.

In terms of how I personally handle these sorts of situations, I've learned to tailor my coping mechanisms to fit the situations I am in. If I am trapped in a bathroom cubicle with someone shouting at me, I can't make use of stimming tools, but I can make use of stimming actions that are normally judged poorly by neurotypical people because I probably will not be seen. I can sit in that stall rocking and flapping my hands if needed, and not have anything to grab and pack away if I have to make a sudden departure. I may not be able to obsessively plan if someone starts following me, but I can obsessively plan in advance in case it happens. I can plan so that someone is expecting a message when I arrive, I can send a Facebook recording on my phone to someone describing where I am,

I can call the police and warn them of my location and the fact I am being made to feel unsafe, or I can even just pretend that's what I am doing. I can make sure I know routes that take me past safe spots and focus on counting my own footsteps as a subtle form of stimming. I basically just handle these situations by adapting my coping mechanisms to account for worst case scenarios that may come up.

It is important to note however that not all of the difficult social situations I have to navigate as a trans woman with autism are quite so vicious or dangerous; sometimes it's just added stress brought into mundane everyday activities. Sometimes I will have my ID refused, because someone might not believe it belongs to me. I've had my bank account fraud locked more times than I care to admit, because business owners believed I was using another person's bank card and ID for a sizable purchase. Having your ID refused or your bank account locked would be stressful for anyone. When you're also on the autism spectrum, it can be daunting to have to go and fight for access to your own accounts, while trying to stay calm enough on the surface that your anxiety handling that situation isn't read as guilt or an indication that you are trying to mislead. More than once I've had accounts locked and, when making phone calls to resolve the issue, had the person on the other end of the line refuse to verify my identity. I gave all the correct information, all the right answers, but they hear my voice, don't believe I am who I say I am or think I sound too anxious, and refuse to give me access to my own accounts. These are normally the most difficult situations to handle: the ones where I know I am in the right but I just can't get people to take me seriously as myself, because of my appearance or my neuroatypical behaviour. While I shouldn't need to do this in order to get through life, I've taken to bringing paperwork with me whenever I go somewhere that I might be expected to produce proof of identity. I'll often keep alongside my passport a copy of letters confirming my transgender status, a copy of my name change forms, a copy of my diagnostic confirmation letters for Asperger's and yet more information tying me to that identity, all sealed up in a small packet in my handbag. It's ultimately not worth the fight leaving them at home tends to cause. I just sort of live life assuming that I am going to have to double, triple, even quadruple prove that I am who I say I am, and struggle with the issues I tell people I struggle with.

In terms of potential support that could be provided for these issues, an awareness from medical professionals of the overlaps between autism and trans status, and the areas where these conflicts arise, could lead to better support in future. There needs to be education that there are unique tough situations that trans people might face, and conversations need to be had about safe ways to get through those situations. While in a utopia you wouldn't need to teach trans women with autism how to stay calm when harassed without causing issues that get them into more danger, depressingly it's not the world we live in yet, at least in my experience.

CHAPTER 11

Learning to Watch Your Friends Die

In the last few years of my life, I have had to get depressingly good at watching my friends die around me. Almost half of transgender people have at some point in their life attempted to prematurely end their own life, and a study by the University of Newcastle[1] found that nearly 35 per cent of individuals with Asperger syndrome had seriously considered or attempted to end their own lives by suicide. While these numbers might from the outside seem shockingly high, they don't surprise me at all.

I am one of the 50 per cent of trans people and 35 per cent of people with Asperger's who have attempted to end their own life. I am one of those statistics; I understand why so many people like me end up on that list, and I have had to get used to the fact that those statistics have not only already claimed friends of mine, but will likely continue to do so for years to come. So, let's talk a little about why I've tried, and

---

1   www.ncl.ac.uk/press/articles/archive/2017/05/autismsuiciderates

UNCOMFORTABLE LABELS

thankfully failed, to kill myself as a transgender adult on the autism spectrum.

Often, when people who are not transgender discuss trans suicide rates, the question comes up regarding whether the simple act of being transgender is in and of itself a factor in suicidal urges. It's often positioned from the outside that being transgender is inherently an act of feeling broken in some way. The idea is that people like myself are depressed, we try to force ourselves to be something we are not, when that doesn't fix our depression we assume that depression is unfixable and that's why we want to kill ourselves. Some argue we look at the changes we have made to ourselves and view ourselves as mutilated monsters. They argue we regret what we've done to ourselves and that's why we have higher suicide rates. During the time of writing this book, an article appeared in *The Spectator* by writer Simon Marcus, suggesting that trans rights charities market being transgender as trendy, leading people into incorrectly believing they are trans and getting themselves into depression and suicidal feelings as a result, and that as a consequence of this transgender people were placing an unnecessary burden on the mental health service that could be avoided by simply not transitioning.[2] Those commonly held notions are nonsense. The aspects of my trans status that made me feel suicidal, and still cause me to struggle

---

2   'Is transgender ideology making the UK's mental health crisis worse?' https://blogs.spectator.co.uk/2018/06/is-transgender-ideology-making-the-uks-mental-health-crisis-worse

with suicidal ideation to this day, are nothing to do with the actual experience of being transgender and everything to do with how the world treats transgender people.

Before I came out to the world as transgender, I held an immense amount of guilt over my feelings of dysphoria and my desires to present myself to the world as female. Everything the world had told me about transgender people told me that to be a trans woman was the most shameful, disgusting act a human could engage in. If I was trans that would make me a gross man who was mutilating themselves to trick men and assault women. I would be a laughing stock, an abomination, a sinner turning my back on my childhood Christian faith. I felt ashamed of who I was, and deadly afraid to admit my trans status, but at the same time I was in a huge amount of pain caused by my dysphoria. I was trapped with two choices as I saw it: live with the pain of not transitioning, or transition and live a miserable life. Both seemed like situations I could not live through. I didn't want to live in either of those ways.

As an adult post-transition, my suicidal ideations are driven by societal views of my existence and the messages those send, attacks and harassment that make me afraid to live my life, and by the rejection I receive from those I care about. To this day, transgender people like myself are still seen and treated as monsters, and it's hard not to let the constant media onslaught of anti-trans coverage leave a mark on my sense of self-worth. Every time the BBC offers a platform to someone like Germaine Greer, explaining that I am just lying about being female because people like me want to rape women in changing rooms and destroy the safety of cisgender women, or the cover story of a glossy women's mag is dedicated to talking about how trans women are secretly just trying to push some agenda that starts with letting women be men and ends with some outrageous slippery slope fallacy that paedophiles will be given socially acceptable status, it chips away at me a little. I find myself exhausted, hearing over and over that I am a monster damaging and destroying the world, hurting everyone by trying to fight for my right to exist.

I know on paper it's all nonsense, but that doesn't stop it reinforcing that paranoid void in the back of my head telling me the world would be better off if I just died. It reinforces that suicidal ideation voice that says I'm a monster. Every time someone attacks me, be it beating at a bathroom door, trying to sexually assault me, tracking down my home address and posting it online, dedicating entire forums to harassing me or just shouting slurs at me from a car going by, it just reminds me that there's a whole world out there that feels so much vitriol aimed at my existence that it can be channelled into these acts. If someone has it in them to hate me that completely, surely I must deserve it? I know it's untrue, but it's often tough to believe that.

Lastly, there are family members in my life, alongside long-term friends, who have refused to support my transition. Some of them just left my life, abandoning me forever. Some stayed in my life, but refused to adapt to my new name and pronouns. Others still just outright told me that I was lying, that they would never see me as female or that they thought

I was a monster. When people who are that important to you, who you've grown up seeing as cornerstones of your life, and whose approval is painfully important to you, abandon you, it can be hard to keep going and to process that knowledge properly. The aspects of being trans that have in my past driven me to suicide attempts, or suicidal ideation, are other people's responses to my existence as a trans woman. It's not being a trans woman that pushes me towards an early death; it's the world's treatment of trans women.

When it comes to autism and suicidal urges, there's remarkably little research into the causes of elevated suicide rates. Speaking purely for myself, the times when autism symptoms have been a factor in my suicide attempts and urges can be explained pretty simply. I live with a head that is filled with constant sensory static. My coping mechanisms are judged; I don't know how to connect properly with the world; I often feel isolated, and lonely, and overwhelmed, and frustrated that I can't ever properly escape this unending struggle in my mind. I will never be like everyone else around me and I will often be judged for that fact. The world is not built to accommodate the unique way my brain works. I sometimes find myself feeling like death is the only way I will ever get permanent relief from the struggles autism causes. I struggle with obsessive, repetitive thoughts that are often hard to shake. If the thought that death is the best way to shut up all the static in my head gets stuck there on loop, it can be dang hard to shift.

The overlap between these two causes of suicidal urges can be tough to combat. If I get a media-regurgitated nonsense argument that I am a monster for being trans stuck in my head, being on the autism spectrum can cause that thought to persist, looping and looping and looping. If I get fixated on how my autism means I will never fit in or be accepted, I can find myself equally fixated on my feelings of never being acceptable due to being trans, and both can mentally boost the other. I already draw attention in public as a trans woman, and if I am anxious about that for my safety I find myself avoiding autism coping tools for fear I'll make myself even more noticed. Both these triggers for suicidal urges compound and clash with each other, and it can make fighting those urges tougher and tougher.

I'm now in my late 20s, and I have not attempted suicide in over five years. The reason I've not made an attempt to end my life in that time is largely twofold. I've improved my life to a point where I now have a reason to want to live and aim for the future, but I have also had to live through the suicides of numerous people close to me, and that has been a very difficult experience. As a trans woman with autism, I have surrounded myself with a lot of people with shared life experiences, which means I have a lot of friends who live with autism, are trans, or are both. When you combine those elevated suicide rate communities, it means I have had to deal with more suicide in my life than most people. The week I am writing this, I've experienced both a suicide and an attempted suicide, both of people close to me. One was a transgender woman who four years prior I spent three days talking through a suicidal episode. One of them was a trans woman with autism who had been there for me in the past when suicidal urges were at their worst.

One of them died as a result of their suicide attempt. One survived, but is currently in hospital.

My relationship with suicidal feelings is complicated and has had to evolve a lot over the past decade. In the times in my life where I have tried to kill myself, it wasn't ever out of a desire to be dead. I am terrified of death itself; the concept of infinite nothingness, even if I won't be conscious to experience it, terrifies my conscious mind. It was more out of a fear of continuing to experience the pain of life than a desire to die. Over time, that perspective has shifted, largely due to experiencing the other side of suicide so frequently. Death isn't painful for the dead, but it is painful for those left behind. Sure it ends one experience of pain, but it often causes countless more. I've been there in the depths of that feeling, I feel no ill will to those in my life who killed themselves, but the pain it left me with is not something I feel I could ever knowingly inflict on those who love me.

Even if I would never act on those feelings any more, I still have to fight those urges day to day. The world still makes me feel like a broken monster as a trans girl with autism, and I still find my brain getting fixated on the idea that the world would be better without me. I'm just thankful I survived long enough to find things to hang on to. The world gave killing me a pretty good shot for a while.

As this chapter has been a bit doom and gloom, focused a lot on death and despair, I want to end the chapter on a brighter note, if one exists for a section of autobiographical writing about suicide. While I struggled deeply with suicidal ideation in my early 20s, and am having to cope with a lot of brushes with other people's suicides in my late 20s, going through my own battles with the beast has given me a real sense of perspective and strength from which to support others in their struggles as an LGBT person, or as someone with autism, or even just struggling with depression and suicidal urges.

My life turned around in an incredibly short period of time. There was a six-month turnaround in my early 20s, where I went from an in the closet trans person, unable to live full time as myself, working a supermarket job that played havoc with my sensory issues, and with no prospects for the future, to living full time as Laura, working from home as a writer in a role where I could control my sensory surroundings. My life really did turn around out of nowhere, with such little warning, and that's the kind of thing I hold on to and try to encourage others to hold on to. If I had succeeded in killing myself at the age of 22, I would never have known I had it in me to be a full-time writer, which has now been my job for over four years. I would never have had the chance to travel the world for work. I would never have met my favourite people, or experienced my favourite pieces of media or eaten my favourite ever vegan chocolate cheesecake. I never would have had the opportunity to dance and play tambourine with my favourite rock star in front of a crowd of thousands, or to become a published author with my life story out in the world. While the world's treatment of trans people may still sometimes play on my mind, and being overwhelmed by my own brain can be more than I can bear some days, I try to remember that statistically, I have probably lived less than half of my life. I've probably not yet met my favourite person or had the best day of my life yet.

I also try to hold on to the fact that my life today is infinitely better than it was even four years ago. If my life could improve that much in the past four years, how much better could it get in the next four? The past four years saw me learn to better manage my autism symptoms, to make friends more easily, to overcome many of the barriers I used to struggle with, to be more comfortable in my skin and feel safer and more at ease with my body. If those improvements have happened in the past, they'll hopefully continue to happen in the future. Things are often hard for me, but they're not nearly as tough as they once were, and I hope that means they'll one day be far easier to handle than they are today. I have faith that my own struggles with suicidal ideation will get easier to manage, but that faith in my own future is just lingering under the shadow of the knowledge that, statistically, I'm going to have to cope with the suicides of people around me more often than most.

Watching someone end their own life because they've lost a struggle I have to fight to stay on top of every day will never cease to be difficult to process. I know there's this idea that those of us on the autism spectrum are incapable of empathy, but it's simply not true. While I might sometimes struggle to empathise with experiences that I have no parallels for – experiences that differ between neurotypical and neuroatypical brains – I have an incredible amount of empathy for, and experience an incredible amount of pain about, experiences I have been through and understand from past experience. If anything, I'm oversensitive to feelings of empathy, as long as I can draw on a similar past experience to remember how it felt. When someone close to me dies, I feel sadness. I remember the bleak unending sorrow, the inescapable emptiness and the chaotic fear that wanting to die is paired with: the isolation, the relief, the anxiety and the obsession. I remember everyone, every time someone close to me ends their life. I over analyse every interaction, looking for clues someone not on the autism spectrum might have caught. I fixate on everything I did or did not do. I picture how easily I could have been the one in their shoes. I might not always empathise with every situation, but suicide is one I sure know how to feel for.

CHAPTER 12

Being a Trans Woman with Autism Is Sometimes Pretty Rad

A lot of this book so far has been about being trans and having autism, and why both those things can be tough, and complicated, and upsetting, and generally pretty exhausting. I'm not going to lie; a lot of the time those are the prevailing feelings I have about these aspects of who I am. A lot of my life I spend frustrated at my inability to be like everyone else, my inability to be comfortable with who I was born as, and upset by the ways the world tries to punish me for the circumstances of my birth.

However, that's not always the case. More than once in my life, I've been asked by some inquisitive stranger, if there was a 'cure' for being trans, or having autism, would I take it? While there are for sure some days I'd give anything for a quiet mind, or the feeling of dysphoria to vanish, on balance I don't think I would want those aspects of who I am erased from my life because there are some real positives to being trans, queer and on the autism spectrum. So, I'm going to dedicate some words here to talking about the things I love about being trans and on the autism spectrum. I think it's important we do so, because if people could start to see trans status and autism as having positives rather than being purely negative, maybe it'd become more apparent why there's such a need for society to adapt and accommodate our existence, rather than trying to sweep us under the carpet or pretending we don't exist. There's value in helping us to live more comfortably as we are, rather than trying to erase these aspects of my existence.

So, what do I love about being on the autism spectrum? Well, while I sometimes struggle to mentally disconnect from a task properly, during the time I am working on that task I am laser focused; it's my whole world. It's what allowed me to write four chapters of this book in a single train ride during the spring of 2018, and plays a big factor in the way I've made my career working as a media critic. I can shut out the world around me and just lock myself into the task at hand, obsessively drinking in every possible detail. It allows me to push onwards with work when I might not feel up to it, and has played a huge role in my ability to remain focused as a work-from-home writer. Without that laser focus, I would have had a lot more trouble resisting the urge to do non-work-related activities during my working day as someone whose living room and office are mere feet apart.

While my sensory oversensitivity is sometimes a hindrance, causing me to get overwhelmed and limiting my ability to get through life, it has also made me aware that I have tools most people lack, which can help me calm down in situations where others cannot. While stimming is usually a way for me to get through periods of sensory overload, the calming nature of stimming for me often works to calm me in far more traditionally stressful situations. I know if I am anxious and upset I can listen to My Chemical Romance's album *Three Cheers for Sweet Revenge* on loop, and the safety and comfort of a known quantity occupying my brain will bring me back to calmness. I know I can pop a weighted blanket on my lap while handling a stressful email, and have less trouble dealing with it. I can spin a spinner ring during a job interview and bring myself to that place of calm focus. For events that for others are stressful and anxiety inducing I have years of practice with coping mechanisms, which enable me to manage these more effectively.

Also, let's talk about happy stimming, one of the most joyous things in this world. Stimming is so often seen as just a negative, a way to get through overwhelming negative experiences, but happy stimming is a thing too, and it's a joy the neurotypical world never really gets to engage with. Sometimes, when I am overwhelmed by excitement, I will just flap my hands, because there's so much happiness I physically can't contain it. I guess the closest experience for the neurotypical community is the idea of jumping for joy. Happy stimming is similar, but turned up to the extreme. It's a cyclical experience, where extreme positivity causes stimming and then the stimming helps to focus on just that positive experience, which in turn makes the positive experience more intense. It's a beautiful nonverbal expression of positivity that feels like it transcends words. I remember one of the most exciting moments of my life, being pulled up on stage by Gerard Way, my all-time favourite singer during a concert in London, leaving the stage and just rocking and flapping and twirling with overwhelmed happiness, and it's one of the happiest memories of my life.

On top of all that there's my obsessive fascination. I've mentioned already that I work as a media critic, and I honestly don't think I'd be able to do the job I love without my obsessive brain and its thirst for information about the things I love. I drink up numbers and data and facts and correlations, and catalogue them in very rigid ways that allow me to pull from a lot of knowledge and talk about a wide number of subjects with experience.

The isolation that comes part and parcel with autism spectrum conditions for many is often portrayed as a purely negative thing, but I like to view it as having a positive: the fact it allows me to be incredibly introspective about my own life experiences. When you spend as much of your life as I do sort of just isolated in your own head, you have a lot of time with your own thoughts and a lot of incentive to understand yourself. Other people for a long time wanted nothing to do with me, and as I didn't really understand how to read other people to understand the problem, I focused on understanding myself to get to the route of the mismatch in interactions. This led to me learning to be very on top of my own feelings, beliefs and thought processes. This level of personal introspection has also been invaluable to my work as a writer. I don't think I'd be able to write with as much clarity about my life experiences, and explain to others my difficulties and unique perspective, if not for the insular introspection that living with autism has afforded me.

Lastly, while oversensitivity to sensory information can sometimes be overwhelming to a ludicrous degree, it is also really useful for being able to feel okay when spending lots of time alone. I work alone from home, and have to be okay with large spells of social isolation, something that many people find exacerbates issues like depression. I tend to find it doesn't have that effect on me, largely because it's hard to feel alone when there's constantly static and noise happening. I can always hear cars driving past which I know are full of people, water moving through pipes that will pass under people's homes. I can see animals like birds and insects moving outside my window. I can't tune out the world, and as such I never really forget that the world exists around me. It's pretty hard to feel alone in a world this constantly loud and busy and full of experiences.

In terms of being transgender, I find most of the positives I have gleaned are less about how my brain works, and more about the kind of person I have become over the years as a result of transition. I grew up assigned male, and as such spent a number of years inhabiting spaces designed for men, full of men, and assumed by the men in them to only contain men. As a result, I saw a lot of the worst of what men do first hand and got a real understanding of how men act when they think women are not around. The terrifying rhetoric and attitudes casually thrown around regarding women as conquests, as possessions, as prizes to unlock, as things men are entitled to, are hard to really appreciate without first-hand understanding.

As horrible as it was to experience those things while not identifying comfortably as male, it has allowed me a really valuable insight into some of the issues that need tackling societally in regards to toxic elements of masculine culture, and has allowed me to help fight for change from a place of first-hand knowledge.

I've also experienced first hand the differences in the ways male presenting and female presenting people are treated, which, while unpleasant, gave me a great deal of understanding of the realities of systemic privilege in society. Prior to my transition, when I was masculine presenting, I felt safer travelling alone at night, I was treated with a great deal of respect, interrupted less often, taken more seriously as an expert in my field and granted more space in the world. Men used to put their legs together when sat next to me; now they spread their legs wide, denying me space. Men used to concede space to me when walking down the street, now they walk in a straight line and put the expectation to move upon me.

Having experienced life on different sides of the gender presentation spectrum, I've learned to understand the place privilege has in society. I now understand better the privilege I possess as a white person, for example, and how important it is to be aware of that, as well as fighting to address those imbalances where they exist, a perspective I might not possess without that personal experience.

I've also learned to fight more for the breaking down of gendered expectations, for men as well as women. While living as male presenting there were experiences in life denied to me on the basis of gender, like dancing and dolls. As a woman, I am often assumed not to be qualified to talk about areas of expertise like video games and computers. These expectations are nonsense; we should be fighting for men to be able to wear dresses if they want to, even if they're not transgender, and for women to be able to engage with masculine-assumed interests without dissuasion. Not every person who wants to experience cross-gender interests is trans; not all of them want to transition, or feel dysphoria, and we should be supporting them.

Lastly, transition has changed the balance of my emotional spectrum in a way that I feel is nothing but a positive. I experience less anger and more sadness, which feels like a far more healthy negative emotion to experience, and a far easier emotion to understand and process. I feel more joy, more glee, more empathy and more love. Getting my body cleared of testosterone and pumped full of oestrogen not only changed my body, but it changed my emotional range to one that feels a lot more healthy and in line with who I want to be.

Also, you know, since transition I feel a huge boost in confidence. I've had to fight for my right to be me, and every time I look at my appearance I get reminded that I got to choose who I am. Every beautiful aspect of me – from my appearance, to my fashion sense, to my friends – is something I chose and crafted. I threw away a me I was unhappy with and crafted a new me who made me happy. I overcame my own unhappiness by revamping myself, and no matter how hard the world tried it couldn't stop me. That feels pretty empowering. If I were suddenly a cis woman tomorrow, I wouldn't have that sense of pride in myself that I had travelled this road and come out the other side the strong warrior princess I am today. I really wouldn't change those aspects of myself, even if sometimes life is hard for me.

CHAPTER 13

Roller Derby

The Intersection of LGBT and Autism-Friendly Group Sport

Growing up at school, and for a good part of my time as a young adult, I stuck as far away from exercise as I could. I was uncoordinated and sports forced me to reveal more of my body than I was comfortable exposing, experiencing more physical contact than I was comfortable with, in the presence of a bunch of boys and men I felt fundamentally uncomfortable in the presence of. The one sport I didn't struggle with on a sensory and coordination front, swimming, became an obvious no go once puberty really started to take its toll, and I basically just wrote off the idea of ever taking part in sport and exercise, be that solo or, even worse, as part of a team.

This all sort of changed when I was around 25, with the discovery of roller derby. For the uninitiated, roller derby is sort of like rugby, on a circular track, on skates. It's a contact sport, where you have one player per team trying to pass all the other team's skaters over and over to score points, while other players try to prevent this happening. It's fast, it's a bit brutal and it's all about teamwork. roller derby is also pretty infamous for being a very female focused and pro-LGBT sport. It's stereotyped in the media as being a sport primarily played by non-straight women, as well as being incredibly supportive of trans women, and from my experience with the sport that reputation is incredibly well earned.

I got into roller derby as a result of another trans woman in my life. She'd been going along to the beginners' training sessions and mentioned it to me. She was nervous about attending, so I said I would borrow some kit and come along. That trans woman didn't come to any more practices, but I went along and ended up having a great time. I say I had a great time; I did fall over a heck of a lot that first session. My balance is terrible when just standing feet flat on the ground, and I had never used quad style skates before rocking up, but I picked it up quickly enough I think.

What struck me straight away about the roller derby group I joined was how totally and instantly accepting they were of me taking part in their all-female sports league. I'd had a great deal of anxiety about joining a sports team, due in no small part to the transphobic backlash often spouted by the media any time any trans athlete does better than their cisgender competition, but the group were nothing but welcoming. Not one person in that group ever brought up my transgender status without me mentioning it first; they were all out waving their transgender, bisexual, gay and pansexual Pride flags during Pride month, and they never made me feel like anything but another one of the girls. One of the experiences I remember as really important when it came to making me feel wanted and respected in the group was when I passed my minimum skills test, and was preparing to move up to main practices with the rest of the team.

One of the things that's done in roller derby, at least in our league in the UK, is that when moving up to main practices, new skaters are assigned a more experienced skater to keep an eye on them, making sure they're welcome and safe and included. This is often referred to as a big sister/little sister pairing, and it was really special to me as a part of bonding with that group. As a trans woman, I grew up being referenced as male, and never got to experience that sort of gender-affirming sibling bond that others experience when much younger than myself. On a weekly basis, having someone pull me in for a hug, welcome me as their sister or little sis and mentor me through those early months in the sport was validating and affirming in a way I could not have expected.

However, roller derby was not a purely positive experience for me, at least at first. It was in many ways a challenging sport to pick up, as a result of my being on the autism spectrum. When I started taking part in roller derby minimum skills training in early 2017, I knew I could functionally rollerblade in a circle in my teens, and assumed that would translate to a natural aptitude for derby basic training. What I had not counted on going into my first session was how much my brain would fight me every step of the way.

When it comes to living with Asperger's, one of my big issues is often audio processing. I find it incredibly difficult to mentally tune out unnecessary background noises and as a result often find it tough to pick important noises out of a wall of sound. In derby there's constantly the whoosh of skates, the screech of wheels as people slow down using T or plough stops, the echo of these sounds off the venue walls, the noises of other sports going on the other side of a net partition, loud whistles and talking, and all of these noises change intensity rapidly due to the nature of quickly moving around the room. What this means in practice is that I often find it tough to pick out important audio commands given in the heat of the moment. I might fail to hear someone shouting my name or derby nickname, I might struggle to understand an instruction shouted from the other side of the room, and the general level of background noise is constantly taking up a part of my brain. The noise at derby is a constant low level static, and I have to make a conscious effort to hear through it, and to not get stressed by it. During the heat of an actual derby game, this can cause some real issues. In terms of gameplay, being able to communicate with your team is vital, and if you miss a shout from them it can really prevent you engaging with the strategy the other players are working towards. On top of that, for safety, it's important you're able to respond swiftly and efficiently to referee commands as they are shouted. If you break a game rule, and a referee shouts your name and number and tells you to get into the penalty box, you have to leave the track straight away or you risk being called for insubordination and ignoring the referee, and being kicked out of the game entirely.

Thankfully, there are some accommodations available that over time helped me to adapt to the noise aspects of the sport. After talking to my team's referees about my sensory processing issues, they let me know that roller derby refs make accommodations for people marked down as hard of hearing, allowing them additional shouts, or the option of eye contact and a visual cue, before insubordination is called. Apparently, while not deaf, my sensory processing issues with sound qualify as hard of hearing and entitled me to additional accommodations to ensure that I was not unfairly punished for failing to hear a referee command over the sound of the static in the room. They let me know that my league, the Women's Flat Track Derby Association, not only support hard of hearing accommodations for skaters with auditory processing issues, like those experienced by some on the autism spectrum, they are also incredibly protective of the right for trans women to skate at professional levels within competitive play. Both of these revelations made me feel far more confident about continuing to stick with the sport long term.

Beyond the audio issues, I'm very specific about the terms on which I am okay with physical contact. The short and oversimplified version is that I do enjoy physical contact when I am able to initiate it and have control of the intensity and duration. If I feel like I have control, and can opt out of the situation if needed, then that is a big part of me being comfortable with that contact. In derby, opting out of unexpected physical contact isn't really an option. Pairs weaving pace lines, whips, hits, blocks and general pack weaving and movement all involve uninitiated and often unexpected personal contact. I find physical contact emotionally and mentally draining:

I am constantly aware of any parts of myself in contact with other people, feel vulnerable and endangered, and fixate on memorising the other person's position so I know I'll notice if they put me in an unsafe situation. I get paranoid about germs and dirt and all sorts of uncomfortable tactile sensory information. I can't do much about it, but it's a reality of derby I'm having to work out how to handle as we move into more and more areas of the contact element of the sport.

Thanks to being on the autism spectrum I suffer with a whole host of coordination issues and motor control issues that were not a barrier to general skating in a circle as a teen, but have been a barrier to overcome while trying to get serious about playing roller derby. I struggle considerably with posture and balance due to my inability to properly predict how changes in balance will affect my stability, my movements have always been uneven leading to notable weakened muscle strength and motor control difficulty on my left side compared to my right, and while I have a lack of fear in the grand sense that allows me to really go for things, small-scale body shifts cause me to panic, leading to me slamming on my toe stops at the slightest sign of a wobble. One stumble and I panic for rest of a given session and my form goes downhill. While I can skate well enough in a circle, walking left to right on a straight line and swapping which foot passes over or under the other with each step is a nightmare situation for me, and one I have had to practise day in and day out at home. I still can't get it right. I also struggle to do things like left-footed T stops or the left leg component of plough stops because my left leg just won't obey me the way my right leg does.

During my minimum skills assessments period, I experienced two weeks where I missed out on big chunks of sessions due to unexpected situations completely outside my control. One week I injured my ankle and could not skate properly, and another week a part of my skate snapped and I was unable to continue skating until I cobbled together a makeshift solution. These situations were ultimately harmless, but both of them left me incredibly distressed.

The reason I struggle with these kinds of situations is they are sudden and unexpected changes to routine. With the constant onslaught of sensory information barraging my brain, routine and predictability are key to me being able to function with a semblance of normality in life. I plan, I predict, I am not surprised and I feel like I have some control over the uncontrollable. I avoid thinking about how loud the universe is on a cosmic scale, where everything is always happening everywhere and I can't control any of it, and I convince myself things are understandable and predictable and controllable. When plans change and I don't have options to adapt, that gets really distressing. That has been a factor in my minimum skills sessions more than once and I hope I can find a solution for that.

Beyond all these, there's also the issue that most of the stimming solutions I currently make use of in my life are not suitable for use mid-derby, while kitted up in derby gear or while actively up on skates. This means that while a lot of these Asperger's traits are manageable day to day, I can't make use of my coping mechanisms properly during derby sessions.

I know this list probably gives the impression that I'm not enjoying roller derby, but in fact it's quite the opposite. I have been loving every minute of my time doing roller derby for precisely these reasons; it's challenging me on a weekly basis in an environment that feels nothing but supportive. Sure I struggle with a bunch of aspects of the activity, but I've been made to feel welcome and safe while learning how to adapt. Roller derby has given me a place to practise working through my autism symptoms, with a fun, challenging goal to work towards while surrounded by some of the most LGBT and mental health-supportive women I have ever had the pleasure to meet. It's a group I don't have to be embarrassed to be gay, trans or on the autism spectrum around, who have welcomed me in as a woman without any reservations, and taken me from a sports hater to someone proud to kit up and get out there with my team.

CHAPTER 14

Where Do I Go from Here?

So, here we are: the end of the book. Wow, this has been a bit of a journey for me to write. I know things got a bit dark and depressing in places, but I want to leave you all on a more positive note: where my life is now, and where it's going in the future.

As I write this, I am a 26-year-old gay trans woman living with an autism spectrum condition. I'm living in a beautiful part of the country full of fields and hills, with my fiancée who loves and supports me for everything I am. I'm holding down a stable job as a writer, making enough every month to live a settled life and have some fun, and life is pretty good.

While there are a lot of unique challenges that come with being a trans woman with autism, and they personally made my life pretty rough for a while, they're all things that can be worked through with a little understanding and support from the world at large. Over the years I've become better at handling my autism symptoms, better at explaining them to those around me, and the people in my life have learned how to better understand and support me with my specific needs. My hope is that people not on the autism spectrum who've read this will come away with that new sort of understanding of the issues, and how to better support the needs of people like me.

I've also got much better at accepting who I am, largely due to the support of a lovely group of friends. The internet made it easier than ever for me to meet other lovely trans people to talk to about how I feel, but perhaps even more important were the friends who met me, never made a big deal of my trans status and just let me be another one of the girls. I really want to give a shout out here to my friends Becky and Makeda who were some of the first people to befriend me in early transition, back when I really wasn't doing a good job of presenting as feminine. They never once brought up my trans status, and just made me feel wanted and accepted in a way that really emboldened me to believe transition was okay and wouldn't ruin my chances of living a happy life. Seriously, if more cisgender people out there were willing to just accept at face value the gender a person tells them they are, assume they know their pronouns best, call them the name they want to be called, not feel the need to make a big deal of their trans status and be willing to defend those friends when they need it, a big chunk of what makes early transition difficult and scary would be improved. If, like me, a trans person wants to undergo medication or surgery, those changes take years and the results vary wildly, and we need friends by our side who will back up our right to just live as ourselves and be taken seriously as women, even if we wake up after a sleepover with a bit of stubble going on.

Sure, living life as a trans woman with autism is sometimes

tough, but those challenges we face have created some of the most caring, empathetic, societally aware, loving people I've had the pleasure to meet. There's something about going through difficult times that seems to give forth an understanding of struggle, and leads people to fight hard to ensure others don't have to experience what we did.

While I personally struggled with early signs of dysphoria and autism being ignored, things on that front are improving over time. Diagnostic criteria are being tweaked to better catch people who previously fell through the net, social media has allowed information about us to spread and become more easily accessible, and children growing up like I did now have better access to explanations of what they are experiencing and how they might be able to seek help. I struggled in a pre-internet age, but the internet is in many ways helping kids like me to work out what they're experiencing earlier than before.

While the lack of discussion of the overlap between autism and LGBT status was a problem for a long time, we are finally starting to see progress. I started writing this book because, for the first time in my life, I came across some of the statistics about the overlap in early 2018, and in the time since my writing on the book began, more and more articles have begun to pop up online on the topic. We're a long way from this becoming common knowledge, or treatment that supports the overlap becoming the standard, but the conversation is starting and I really hope this book serves as a catalyst to get this conversation spreading.

Coming out of the closet as LGBT is still difficult, as is coming to terms with being on the autism spectrum, but with the internet age firmly upon us, children today have more role models to encourage them than ever before. From rock stars to actresses, YouTube stars to professional gamers, there are idols out there kids can look to, and just be reminded that being trans and having autism are not necessarily barriers to achieving your dreams and living a happy life. While transition can be tough for people on the autism spectrum, there are constantly more and more advice, tools, clothing and communities available to help find ways through those turbulent years without setting off sensory issues. The fact that I own seam-free clothing and stimming jewellery is a sign we're slowly making progress.

While a lot of LGBT spaces are still not accommodating to adults with autism, the fact that Pride events are attempting to create spaces and London is soon to be home to a dedicated space for adults on the autism spectrum is a reassuring sign that there's an awareness of the needs of the community.

Sure, things still suck sometimes. I'm having to get more comfortable than I would like about death and I'm occasionally judged by the world for trying to squeeze some childhood into my late 20s, but I feel proud enough of myself to no longer hide who I am.

My name is Laura, and I am a trans woman living with autism. My road to where I am today has been rocky to say the least, but I wouldn't be who I am without the things that make me me.

I am proud to be a trans woman with autism, and no matter what the world tries, it's not getting rid of me.

Further Resources

Now that my story is done, at least for now, some of you might be left wanting more information on some of the things I've talked about. This section of the book aims to direct you to some resources that might be useful to engage with. The following suggestions are in no way required reading, but they're things you might find useful or informative after reading this book.

A Disproportionate Number of Autistic Youth Are Transgender. Why? by Evan Urquhart, *Slate*, https://slate.com/human-interest/2018/03/why-are-a-disproportionate-number-of-autistic-youth-transgender.html

Gender and Autism, The National Autistic Society, www.autism.org.uk/about/what-is/gender.aspx

Life on the Autism Spectrum: A Guide for Girls and Women by Karen McKibbin (Jessica Kingsley Publishers)

GLAAD Media Reference Guide: Transgender, www.glaad.
org/reference/transgender

Mermaids, a charity dedicated to supporting transgender
youth, www.mermaidsuk.org.uk

Transgender 101: A Guide to Gender and Identity to Help You
Keep Up with the Conversation by Sam Dylan Finch, https://
everydayfeminism.com/2016/08/transgender-101

What is Asperger Syndrome? The National Autistic Society,
www.autism.org.uk/about/what-is/asperger.aspx

*Women and Girls with Autism Spectrum Disorder:
Understanding Life Experiences from Early Childhood to Old
Age* by Sarah Hendrickx (Jessica Kingsley Publishers)